welcome SUGAR SKULLS COLORING BOOK

YOU HAVE THE ART

RENATA IGLESIAS

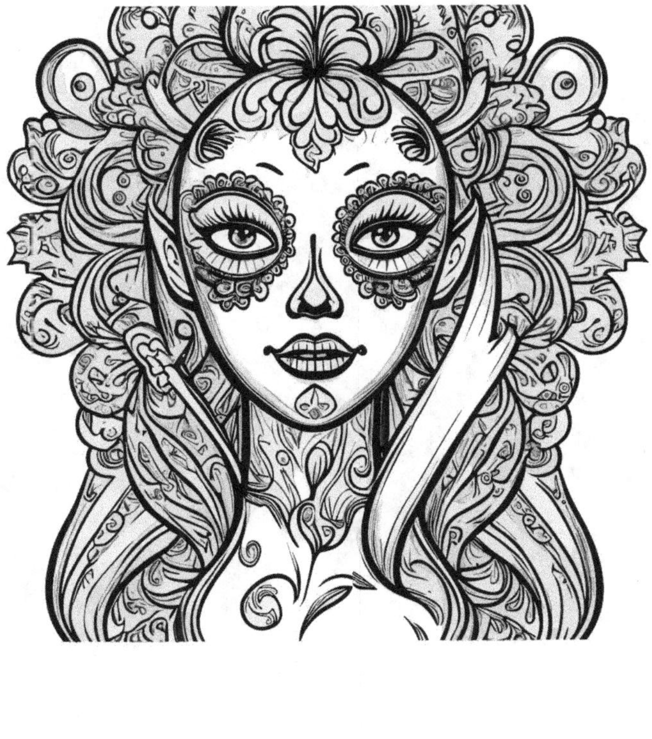

ESTE LIBRO PERTENECE A:

____

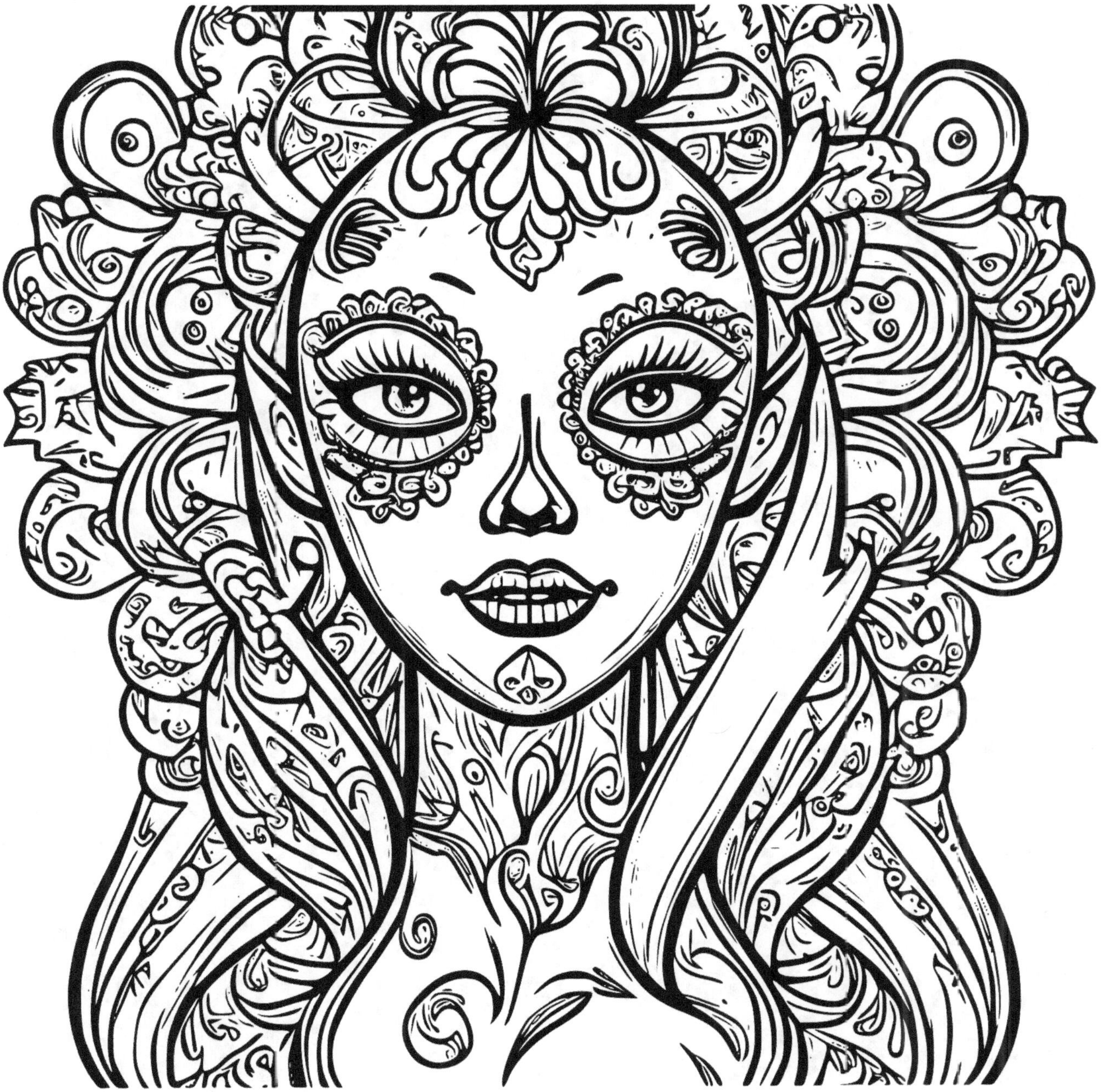

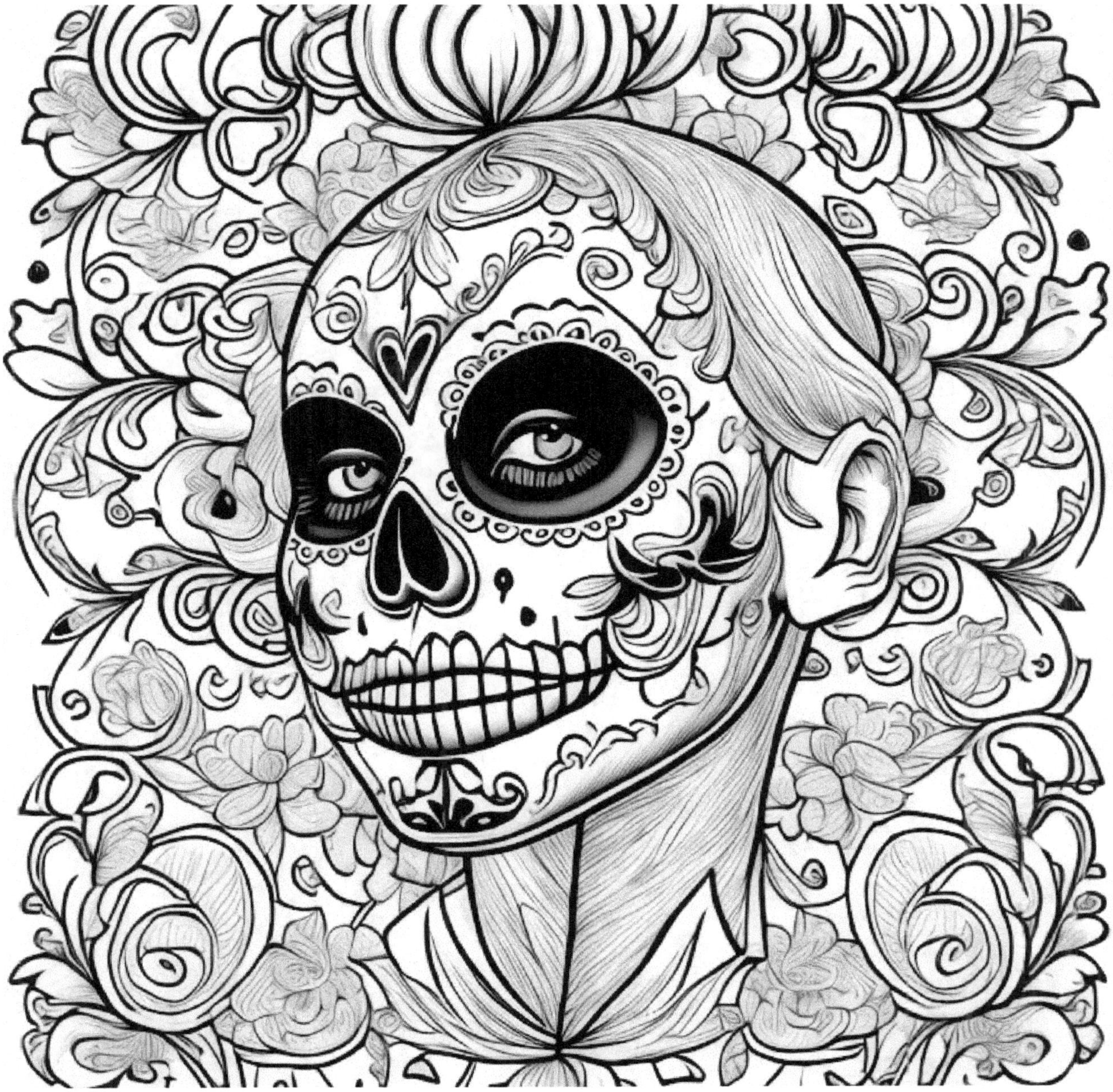

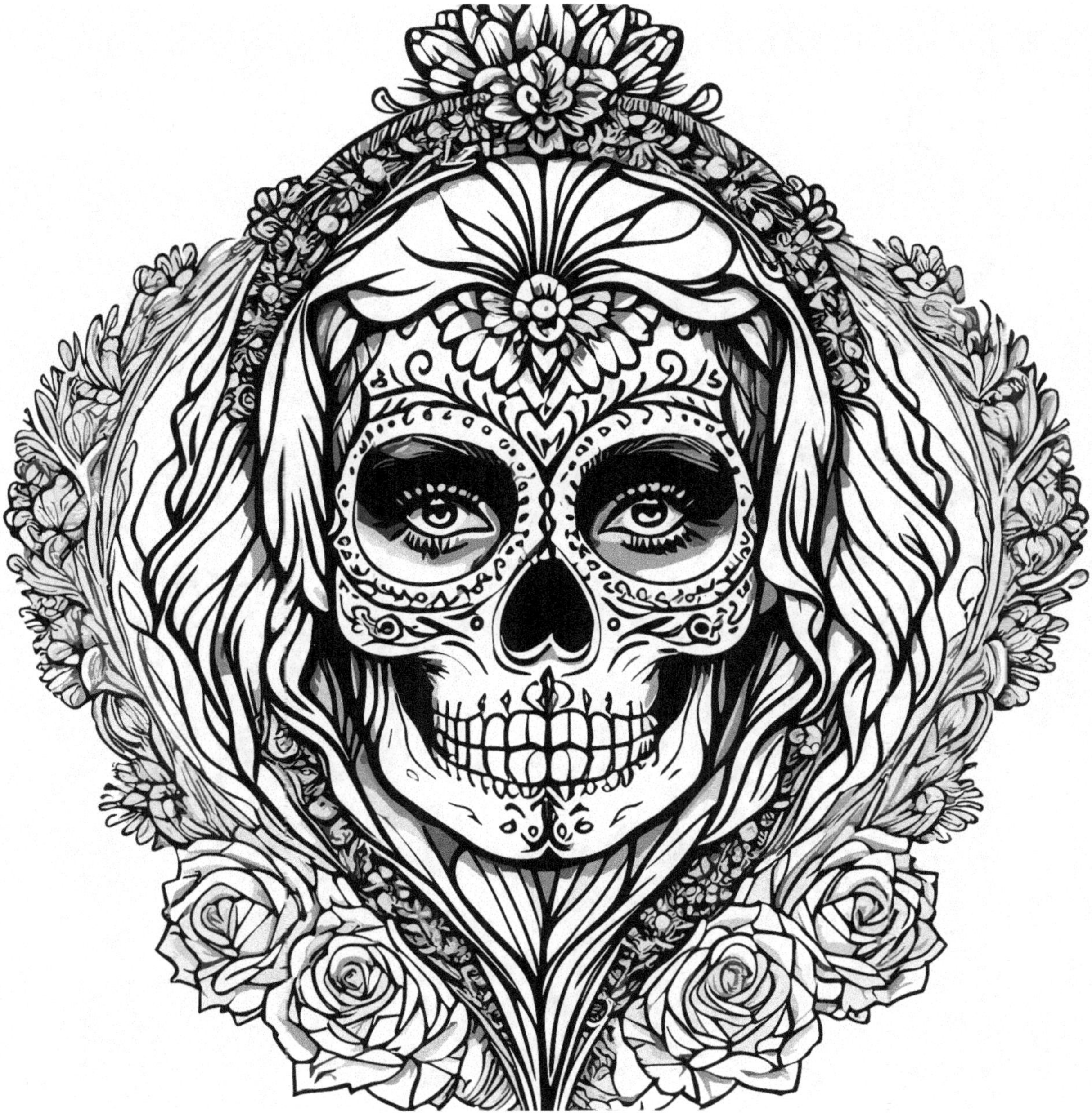

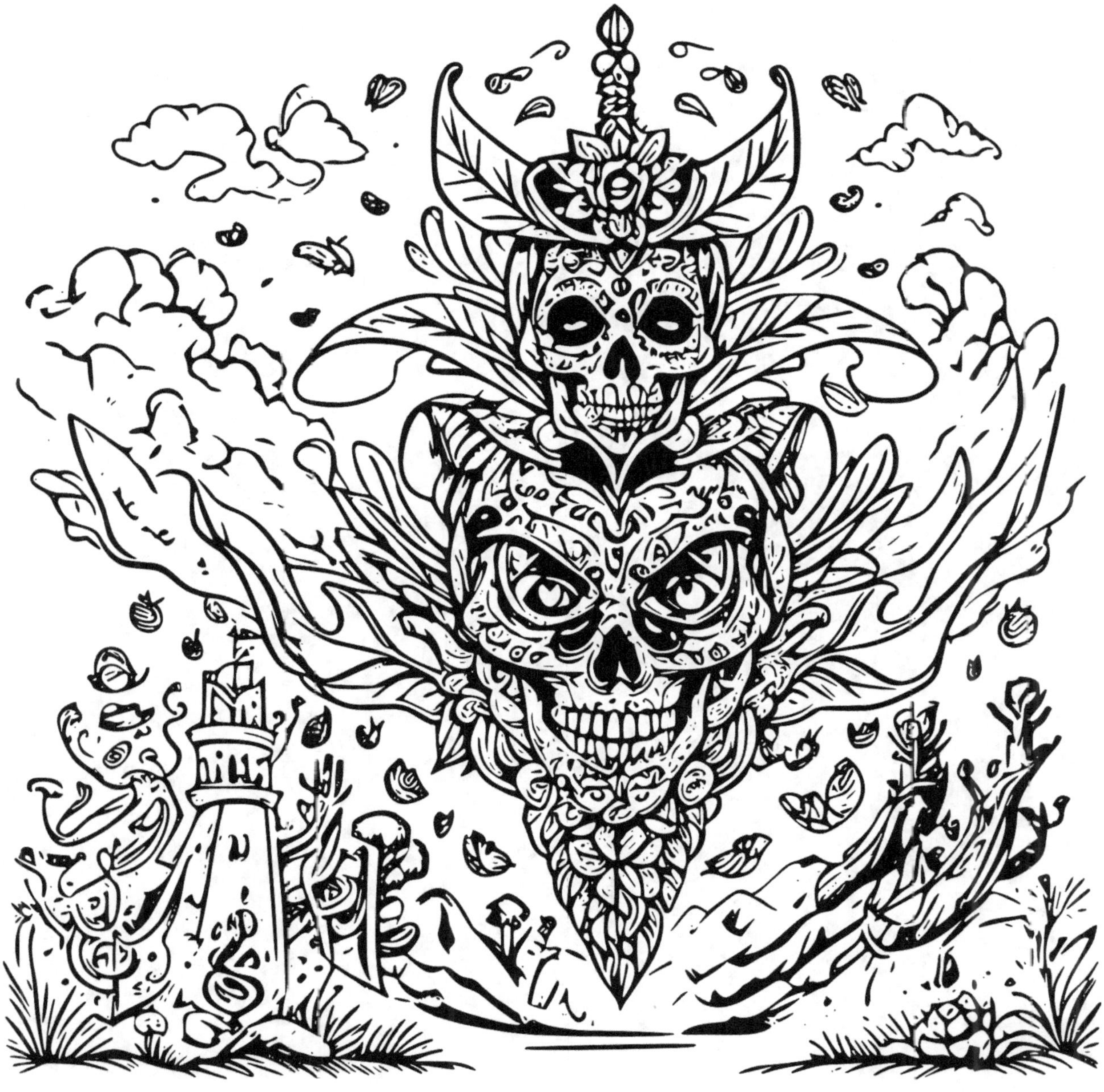

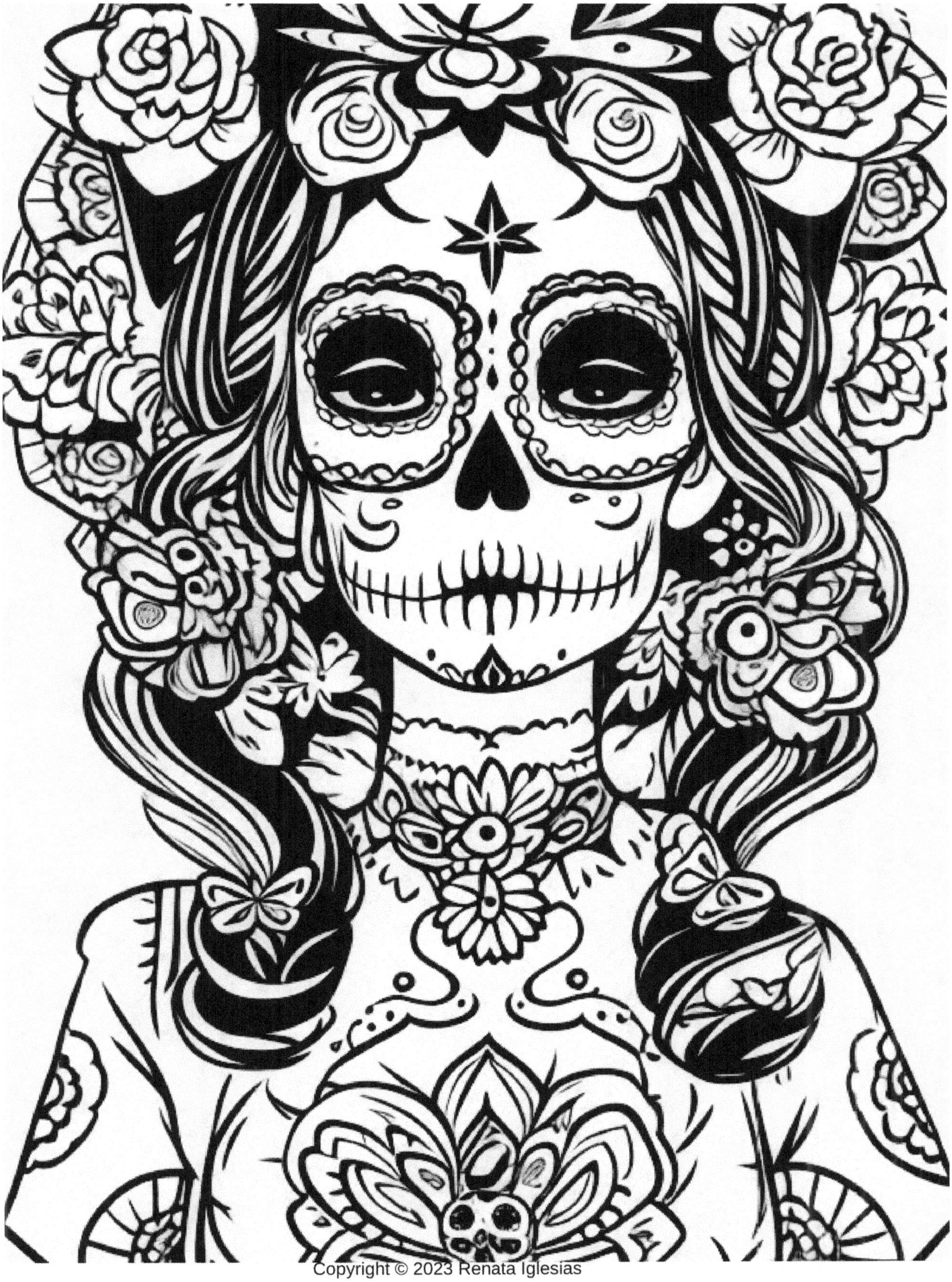

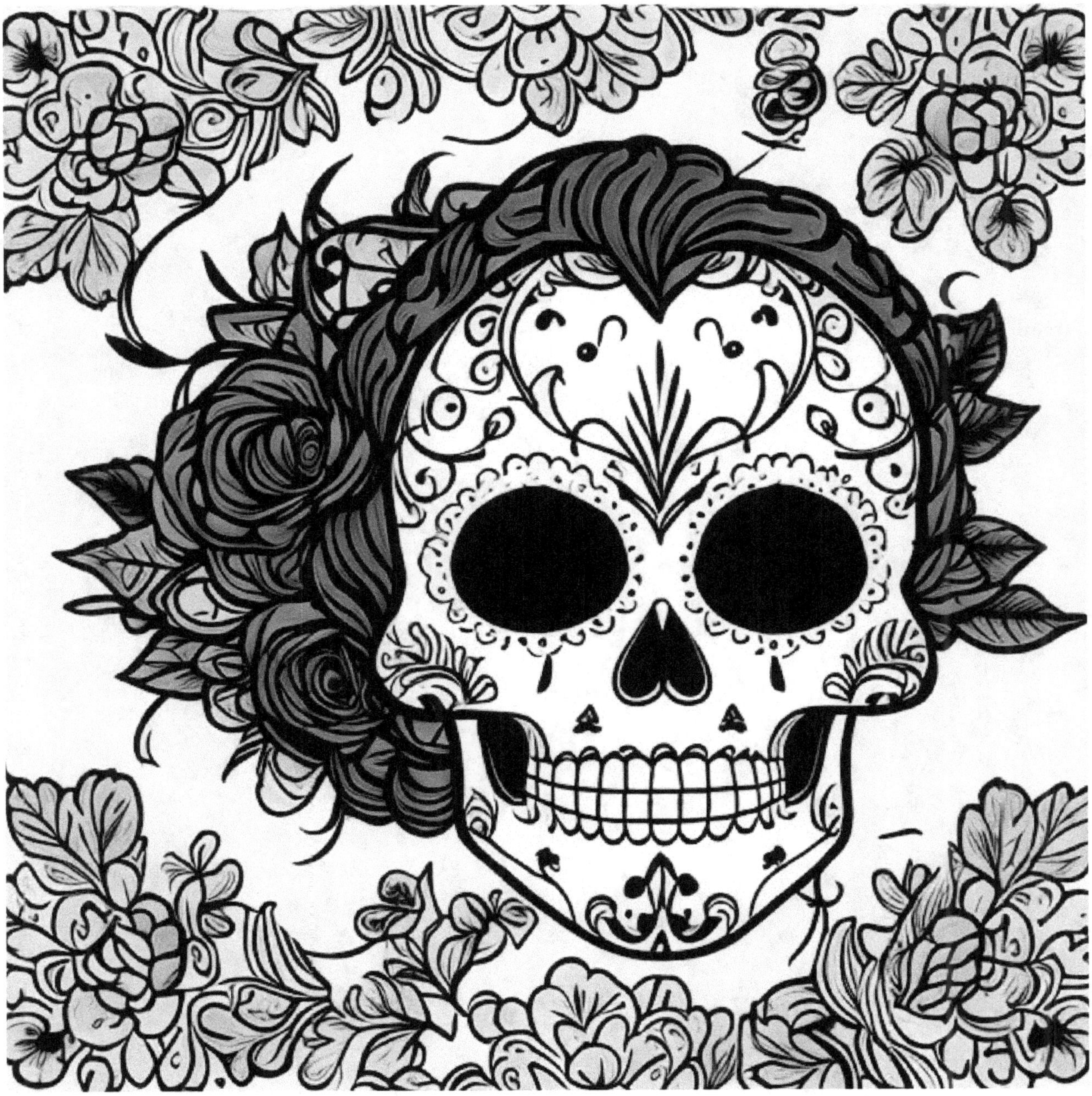

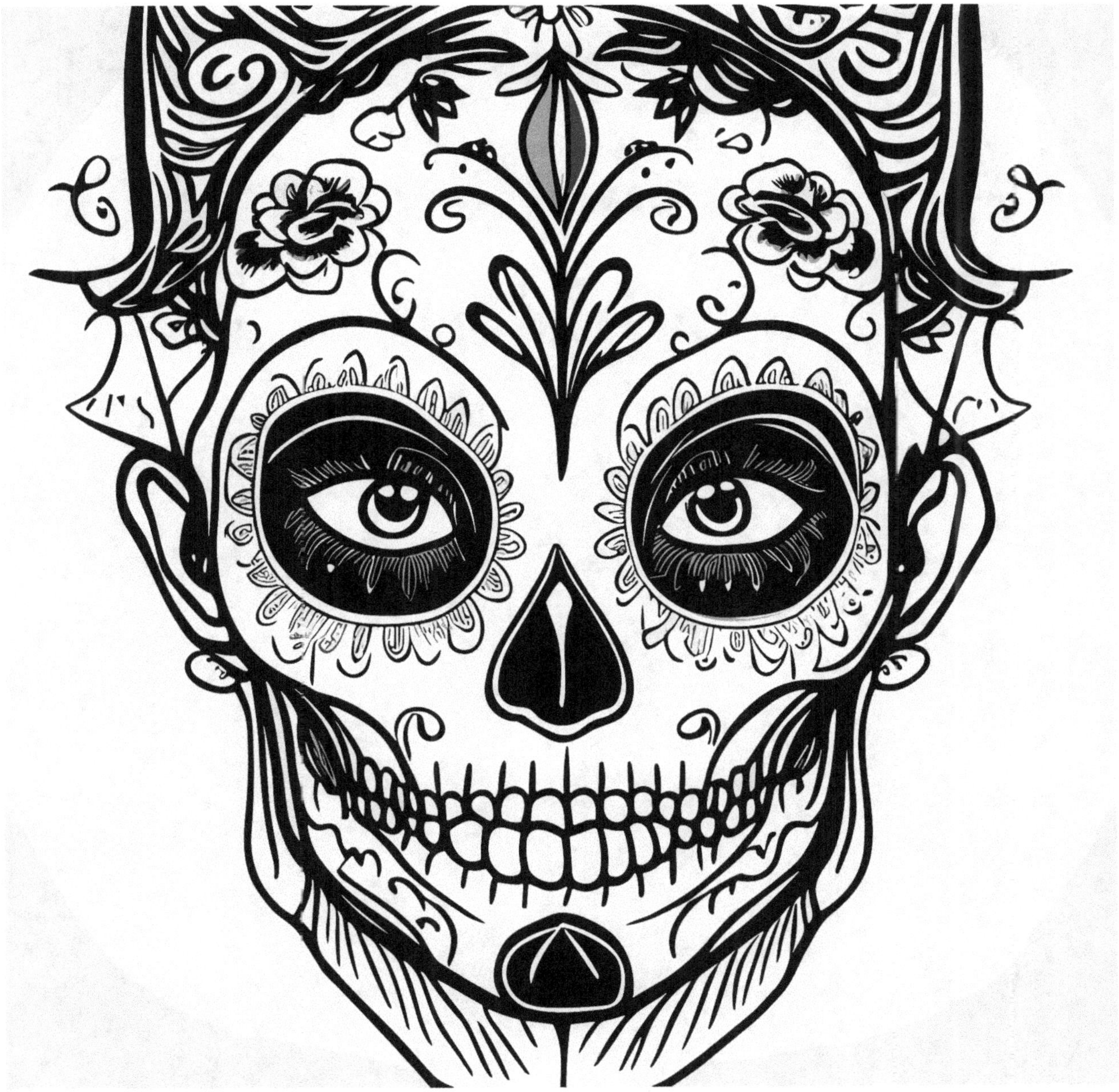

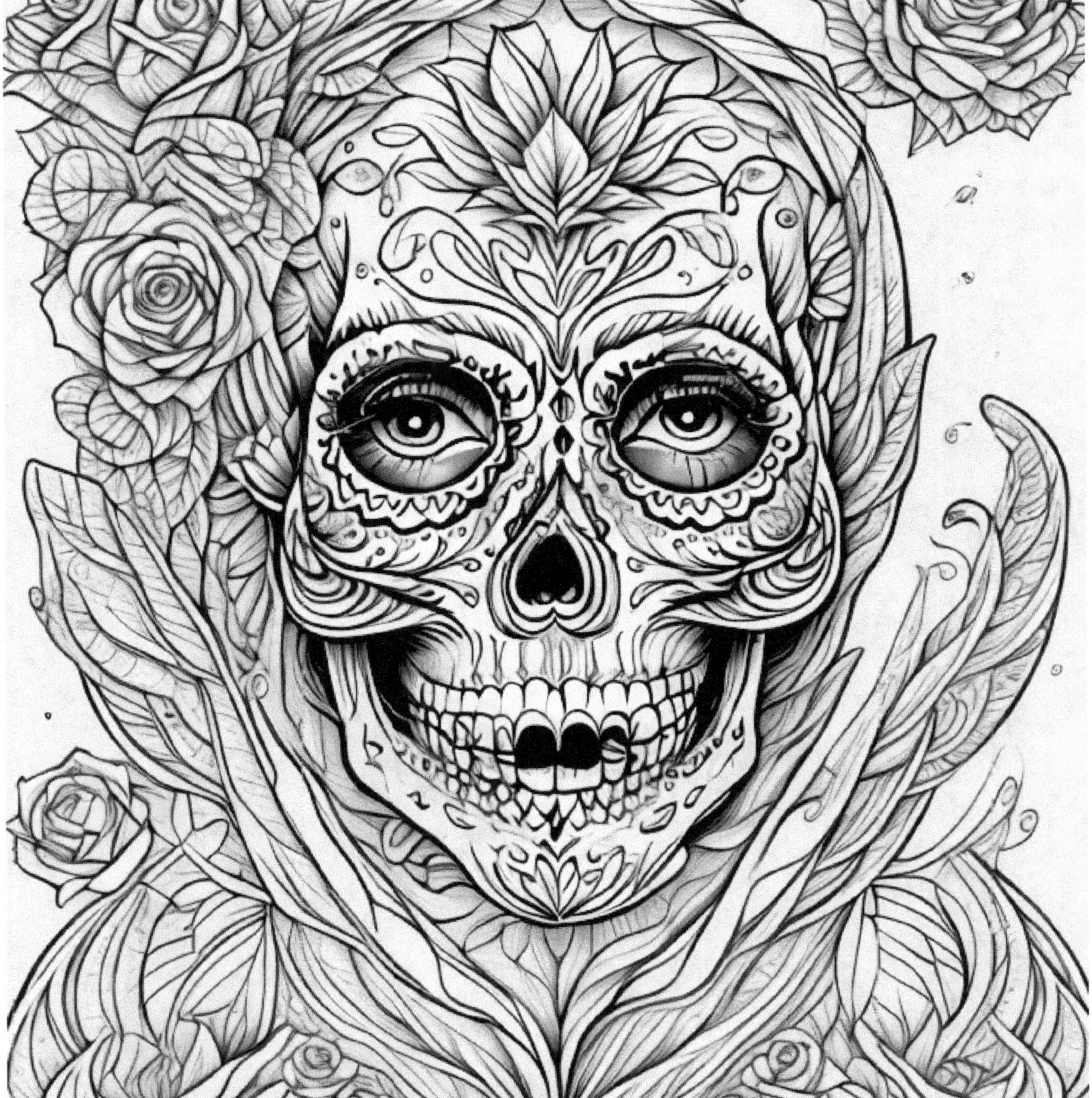

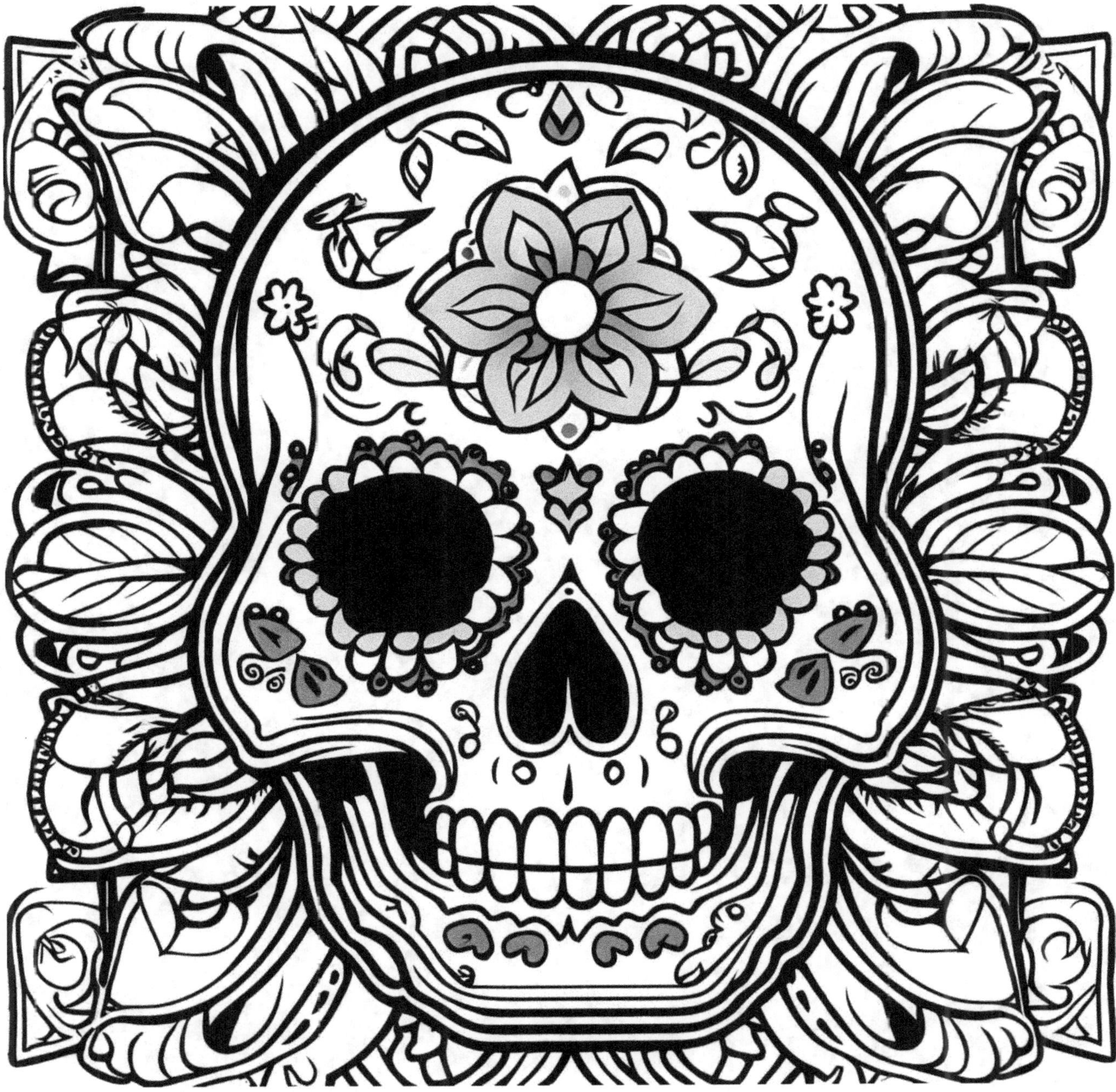

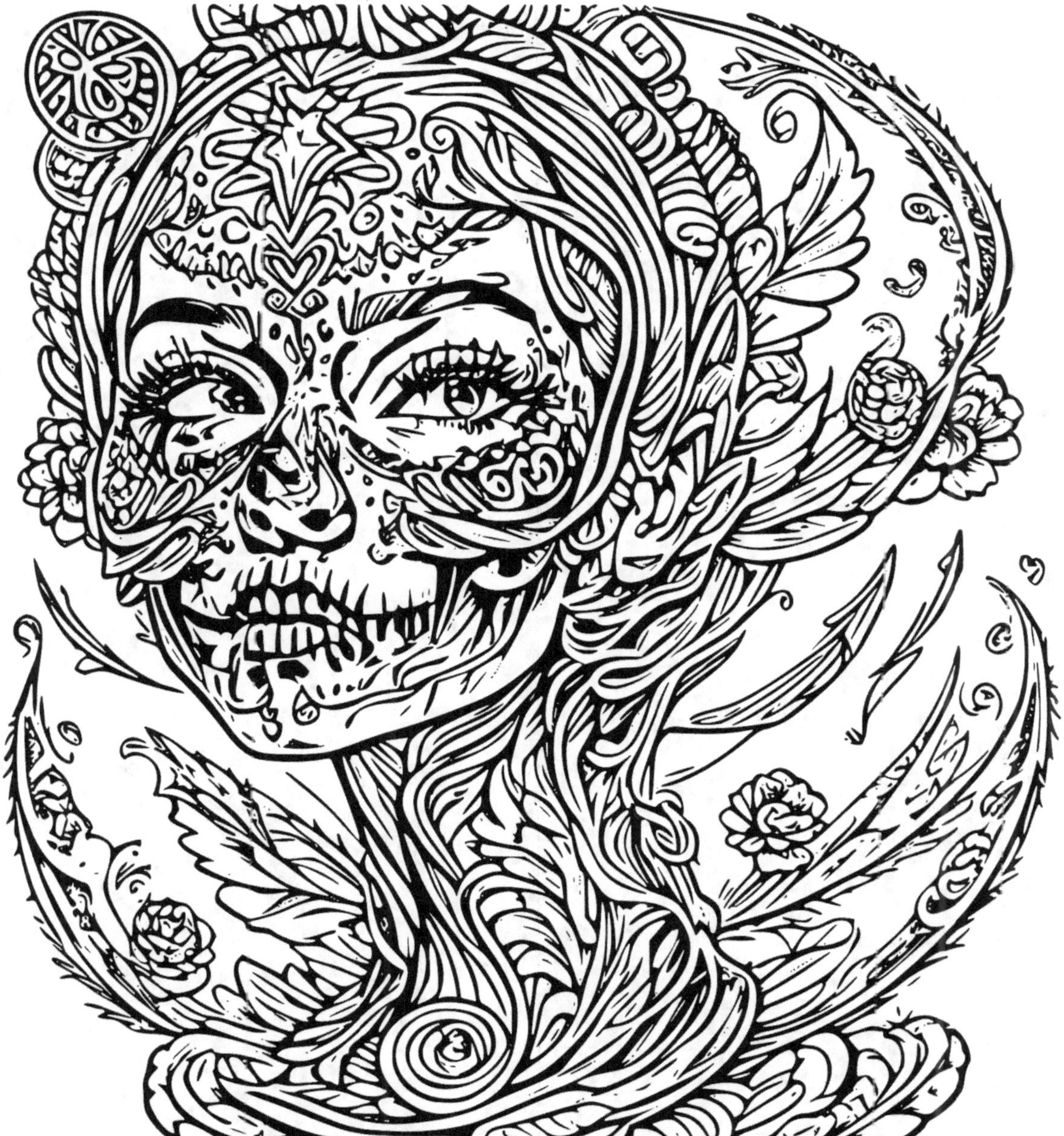

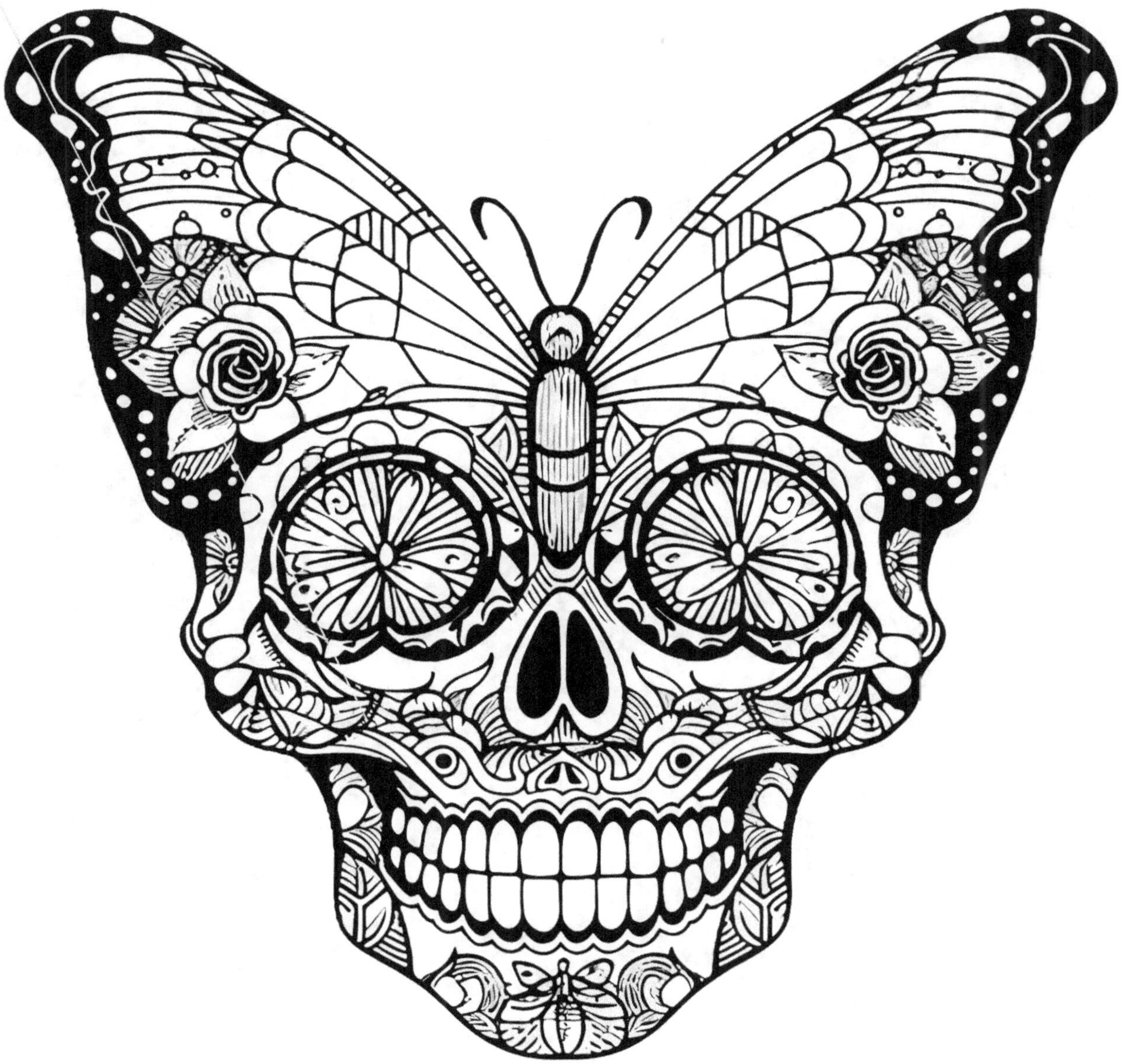

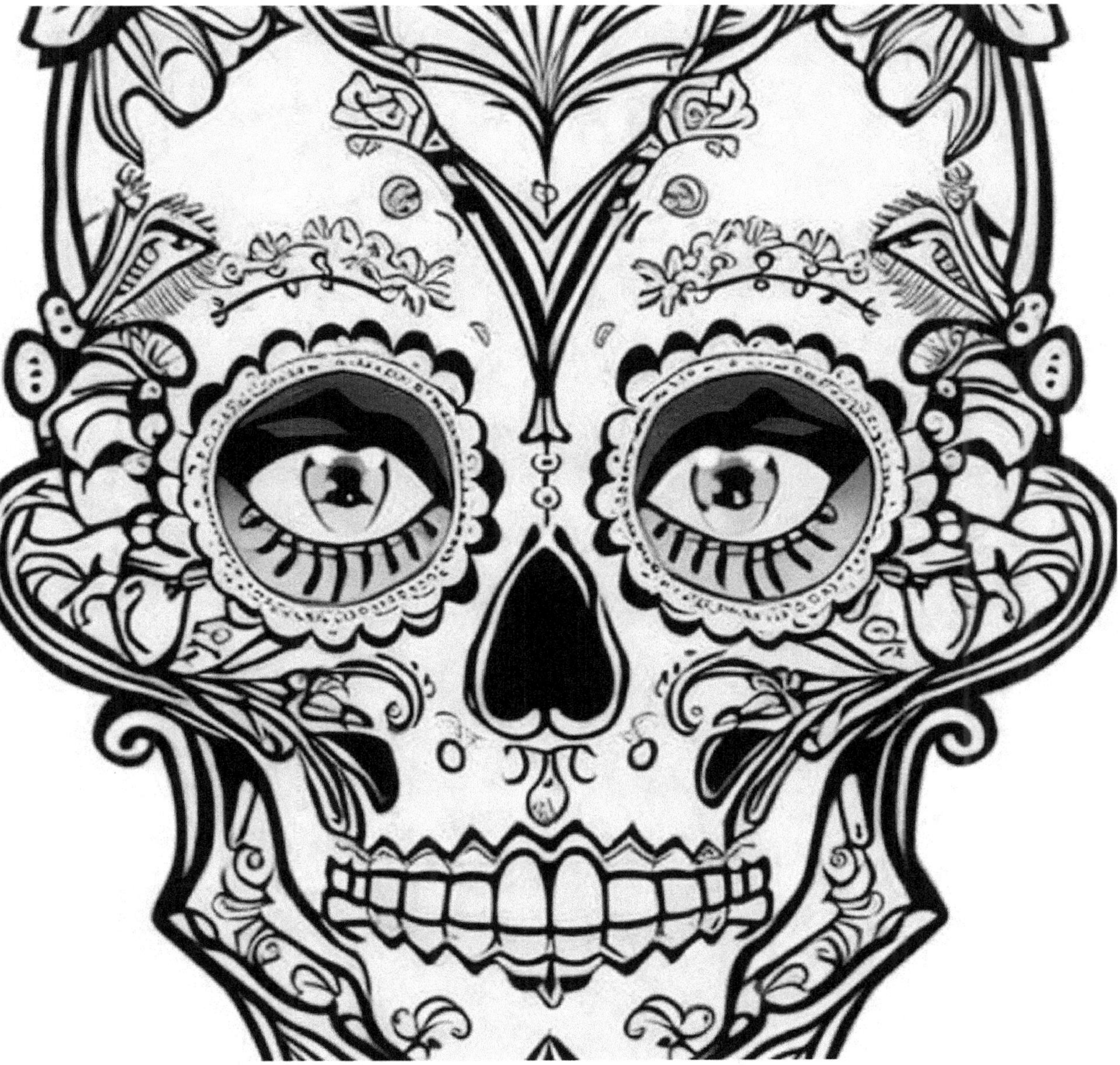

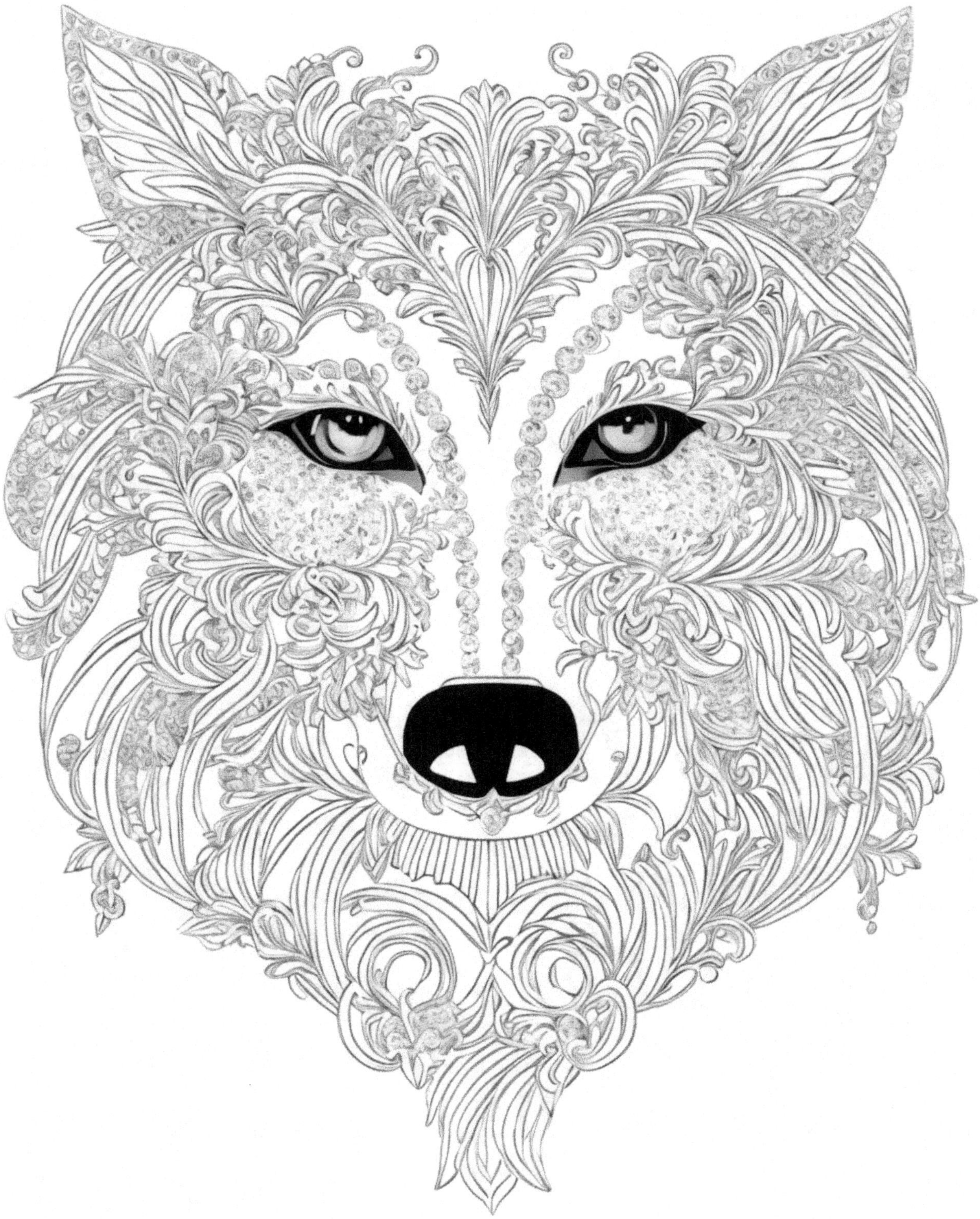

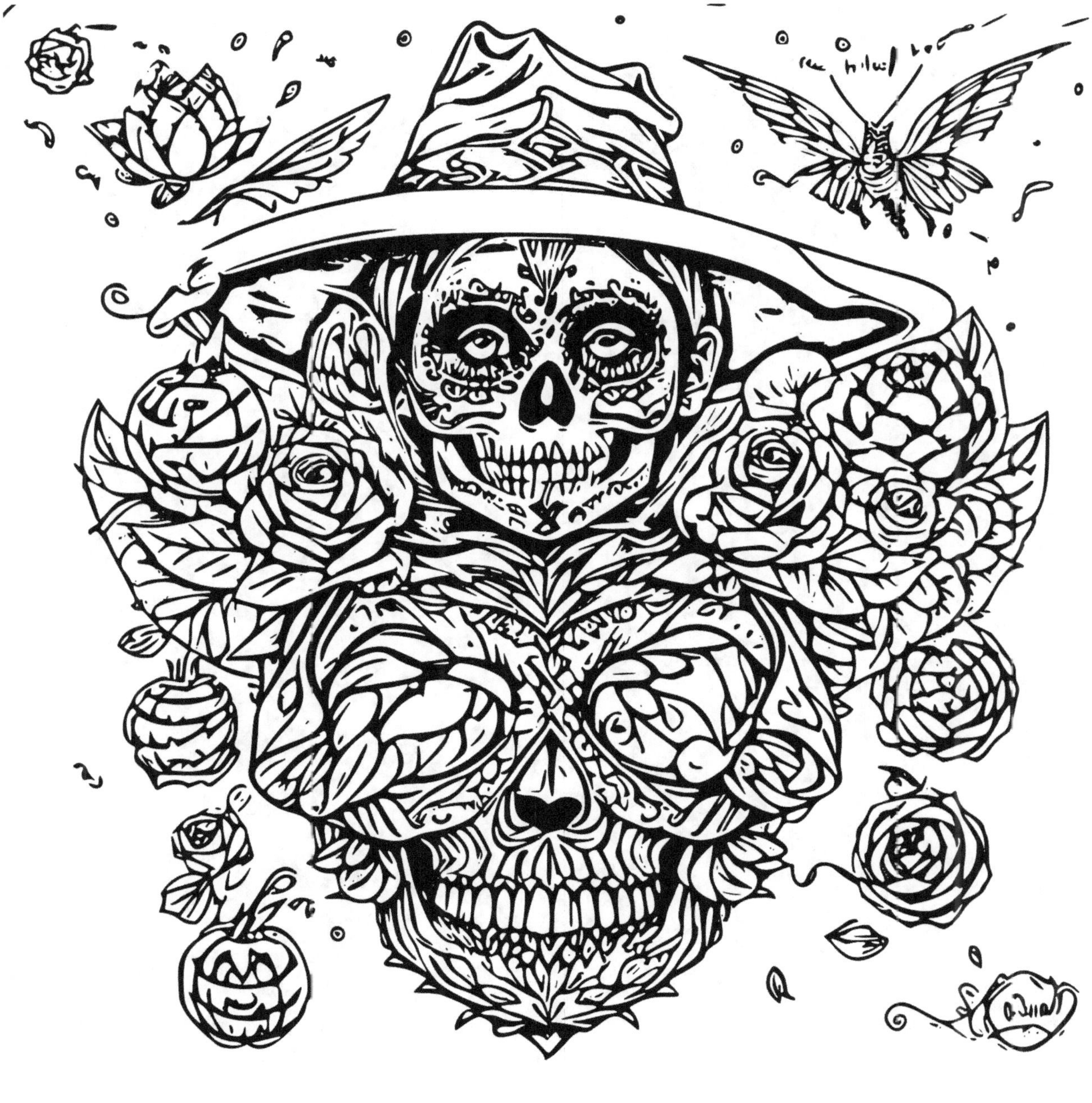

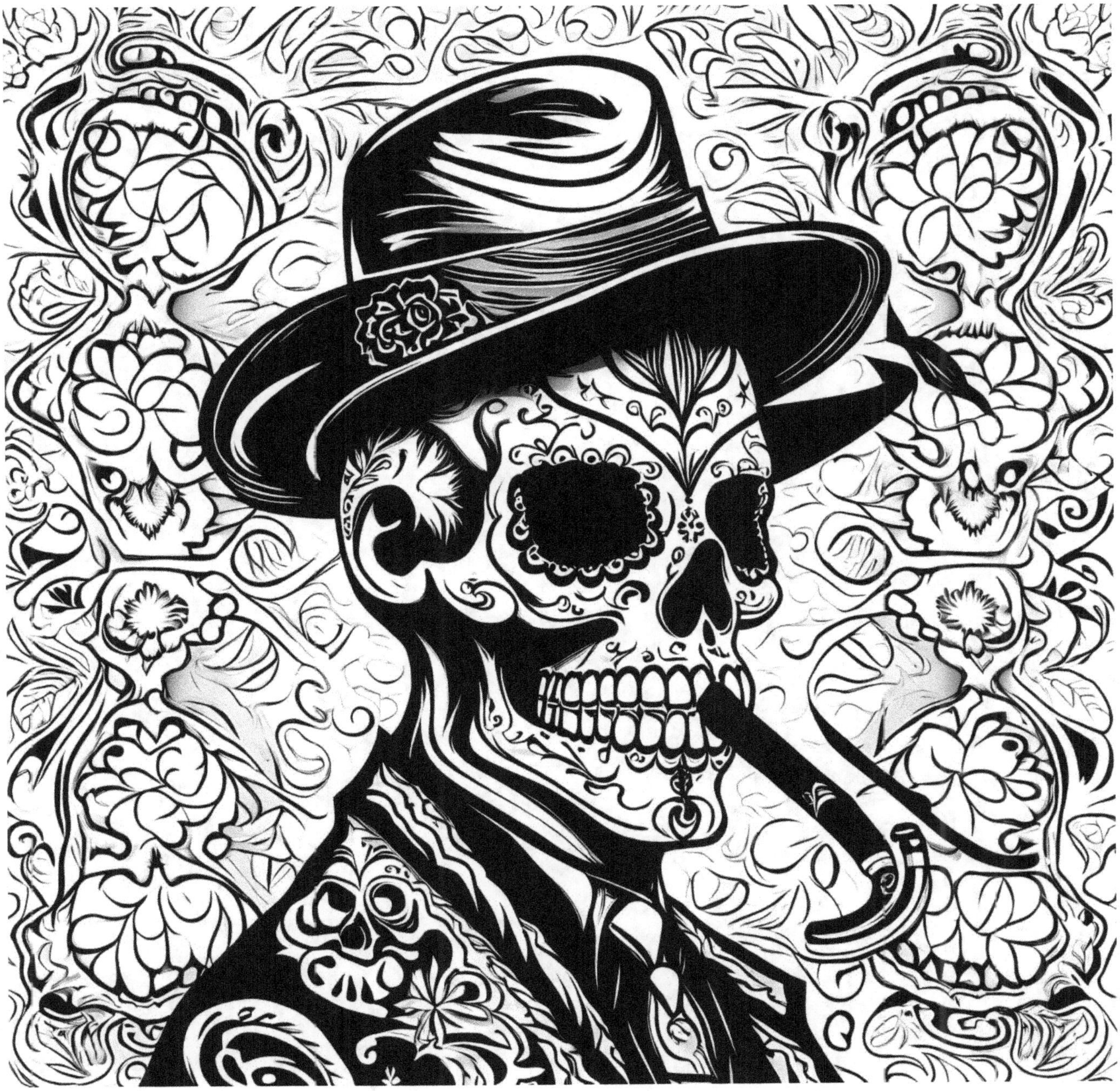

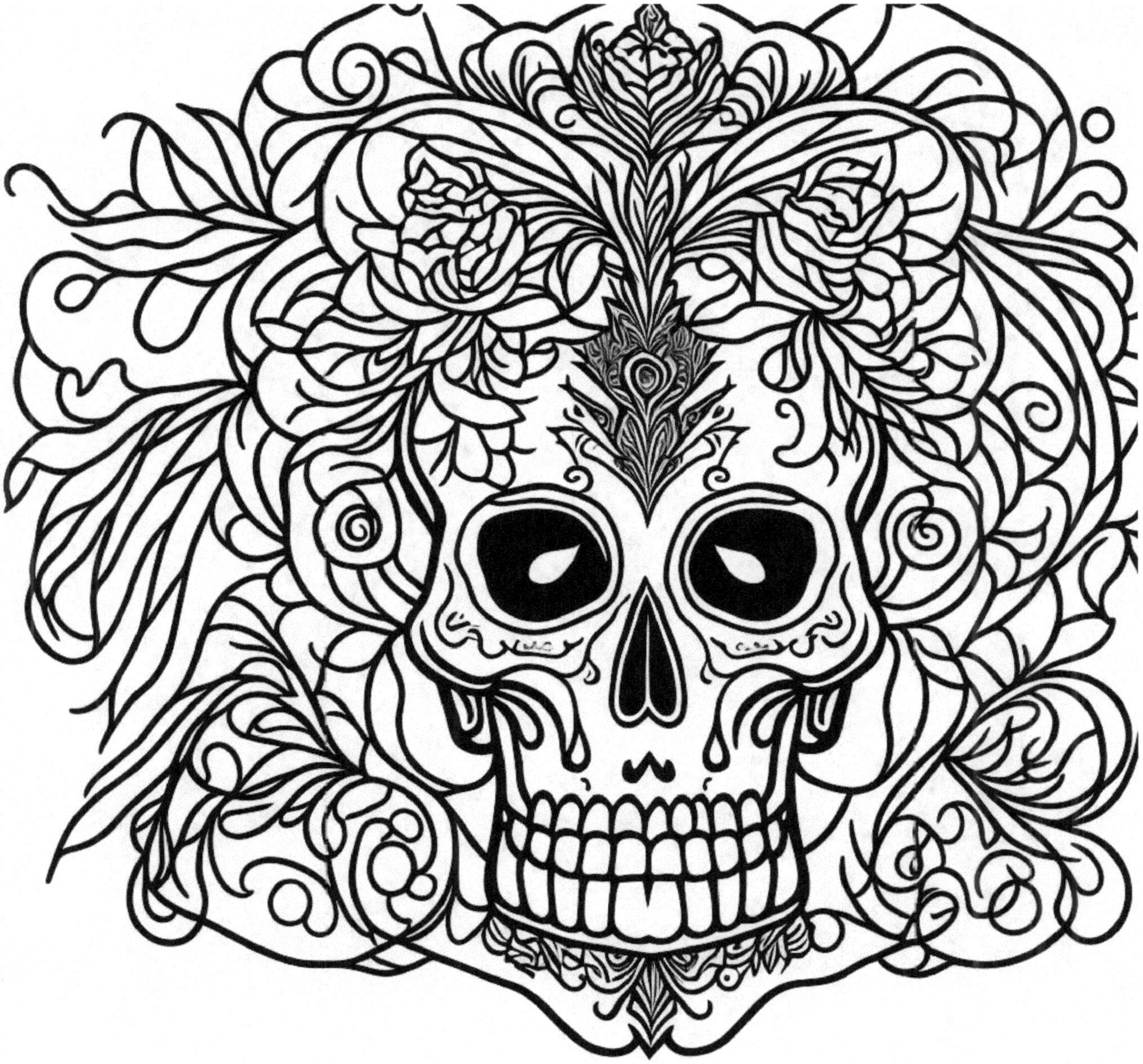

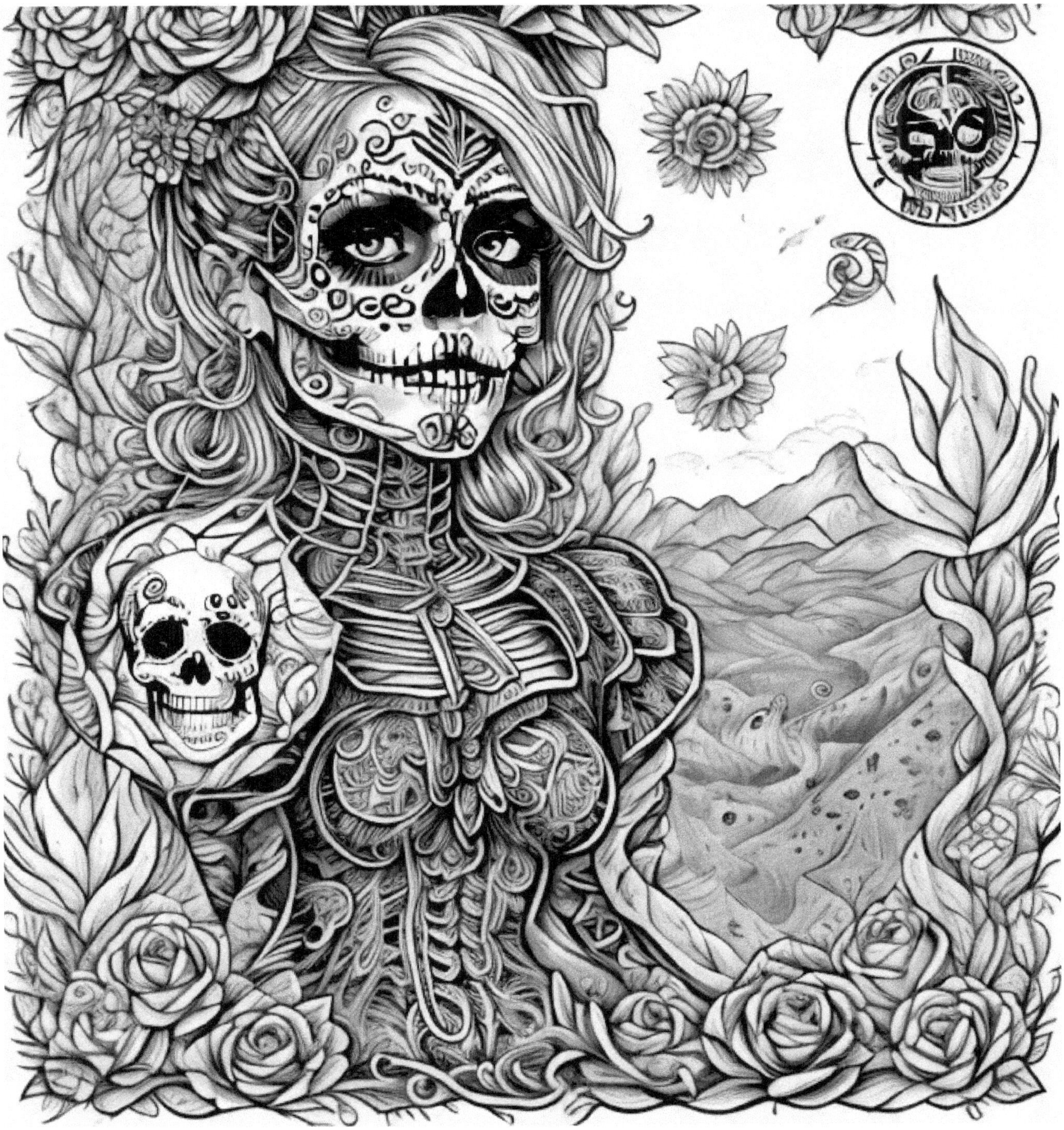

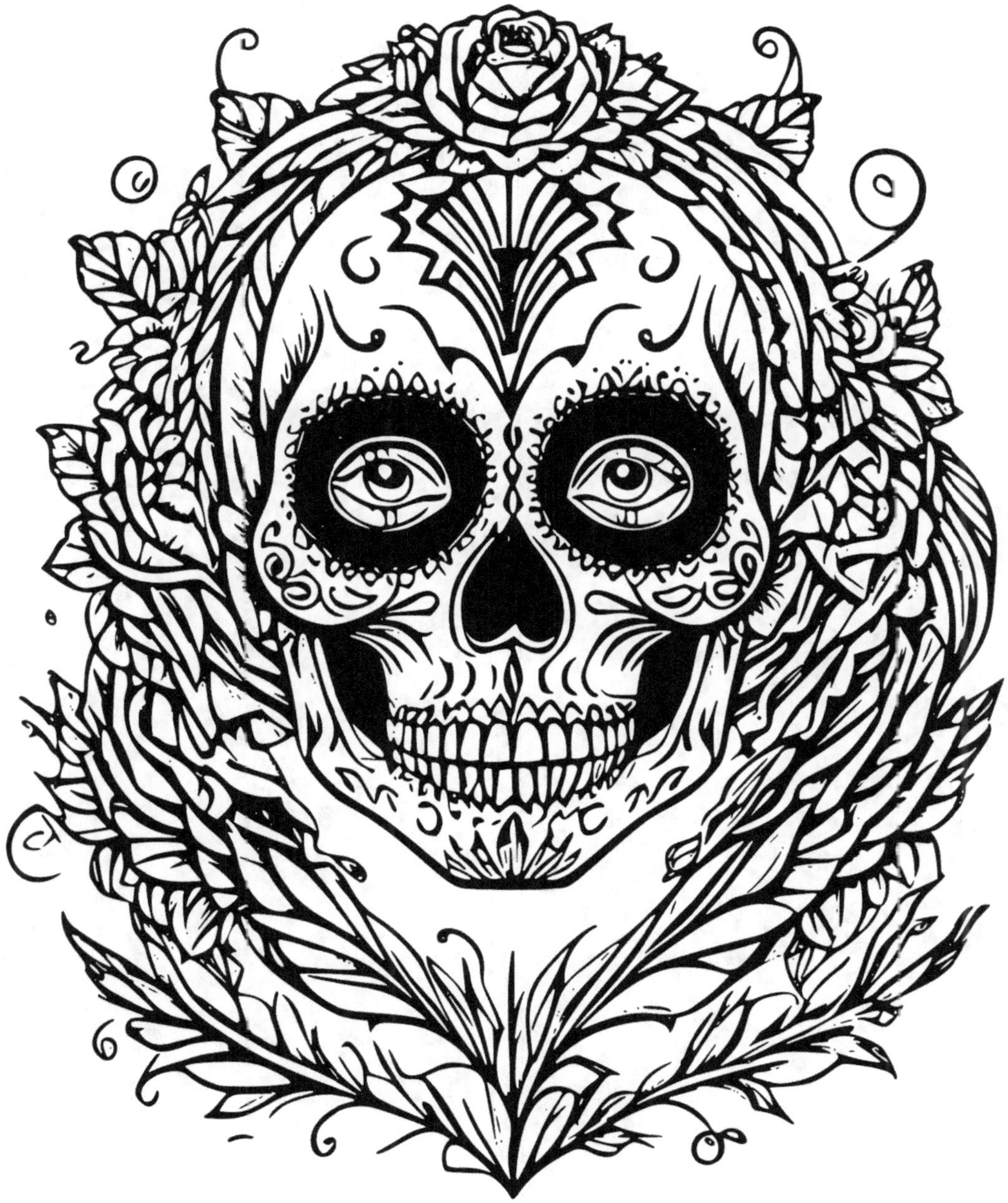

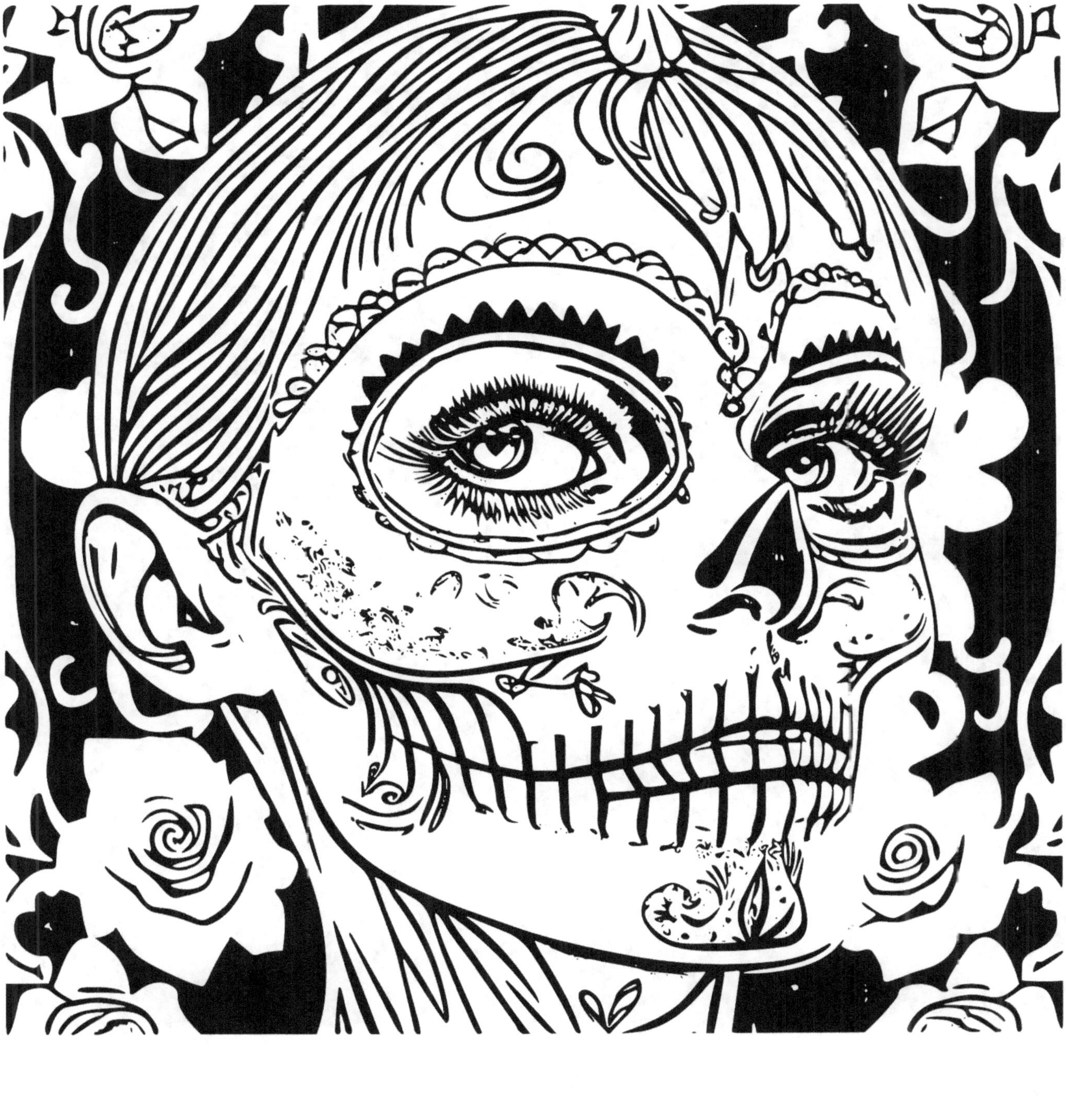

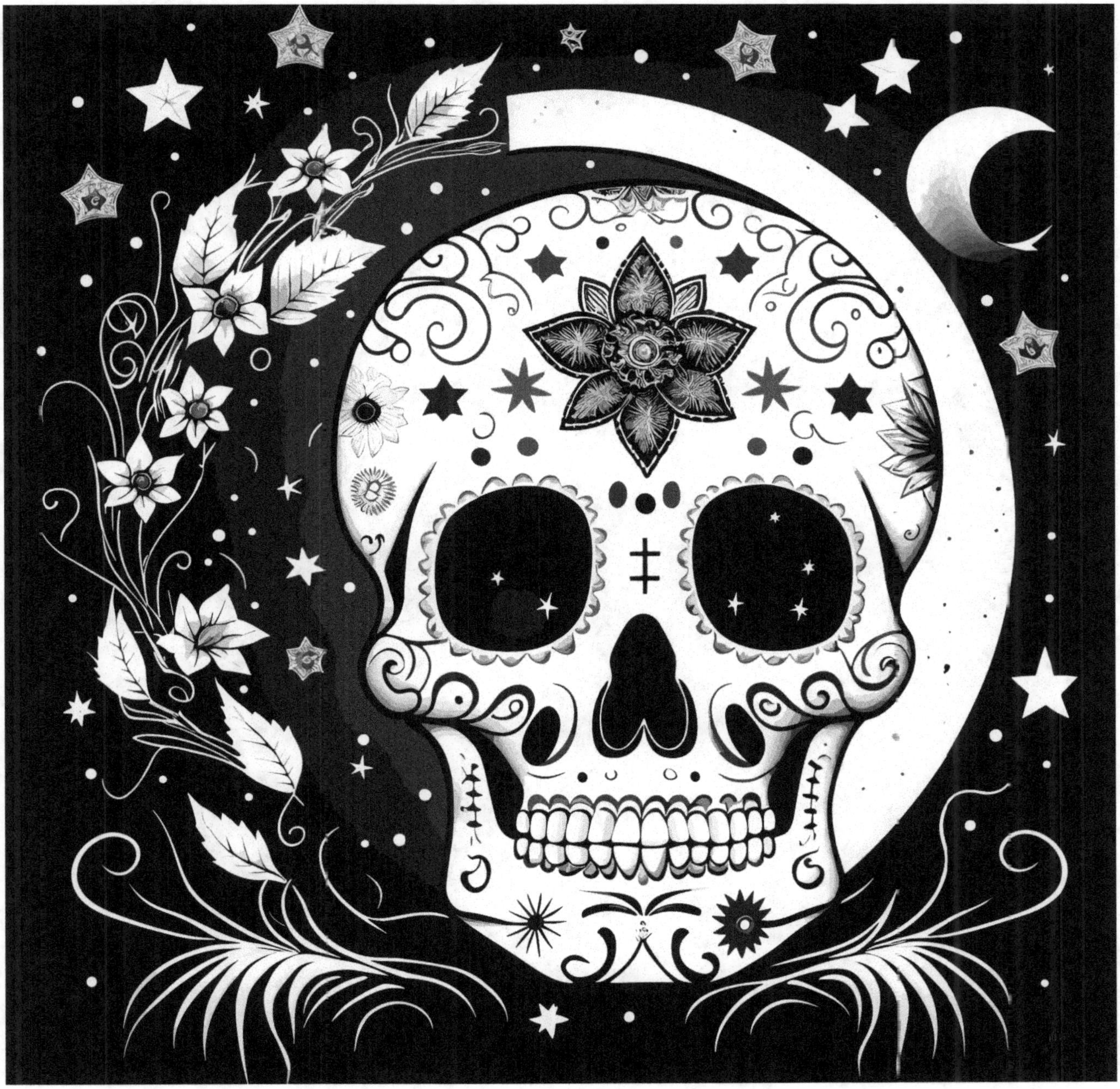

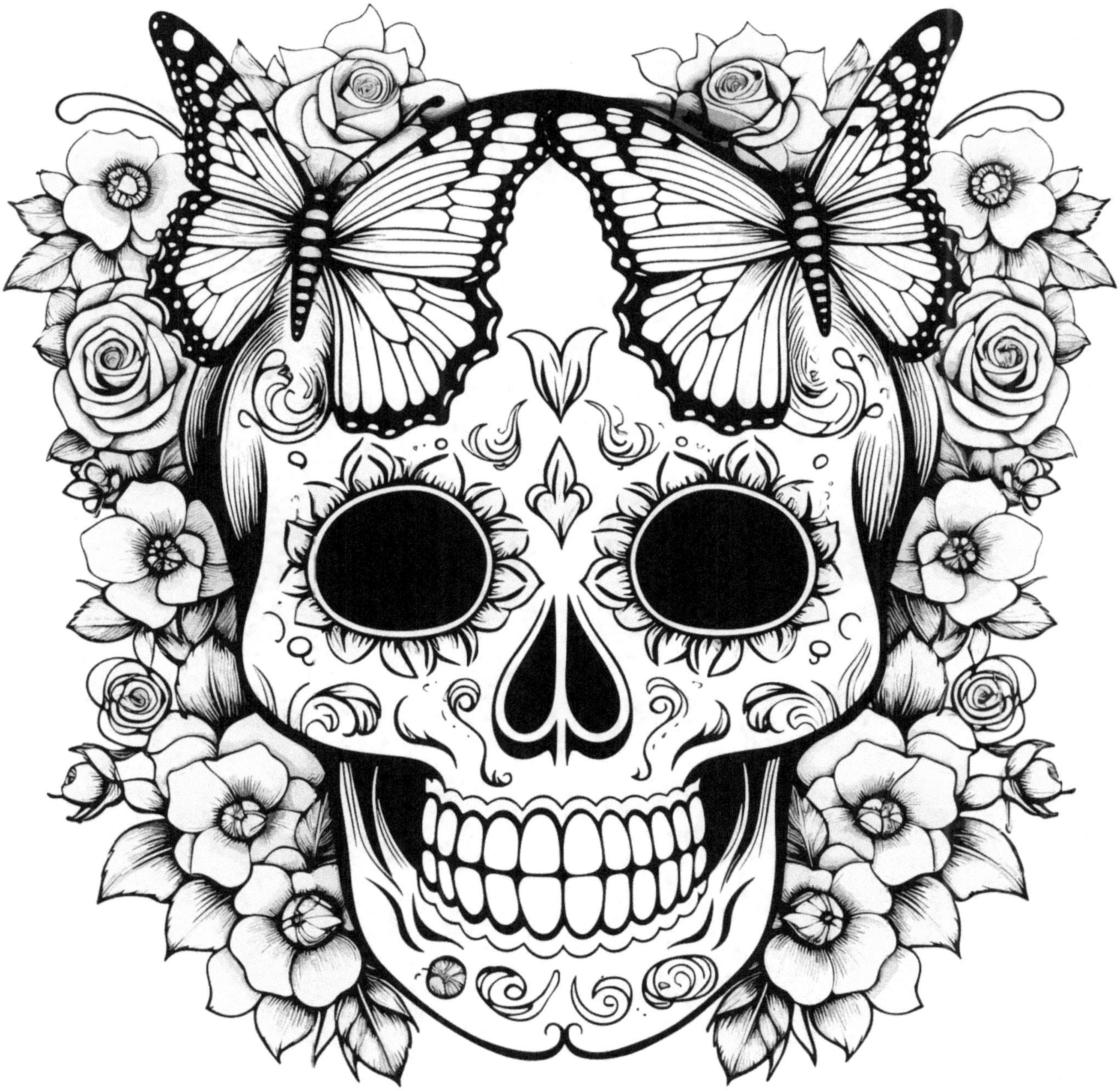

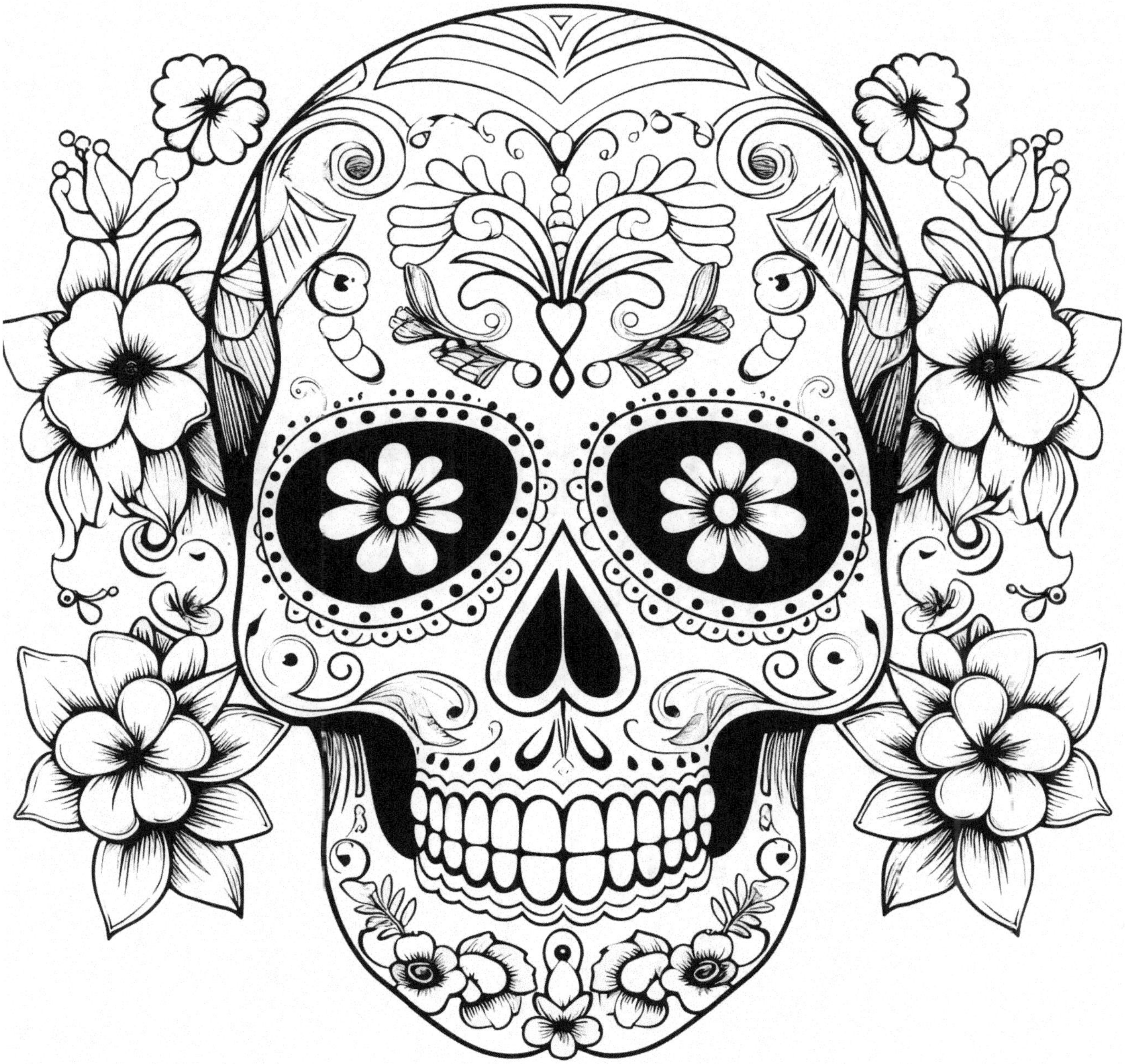

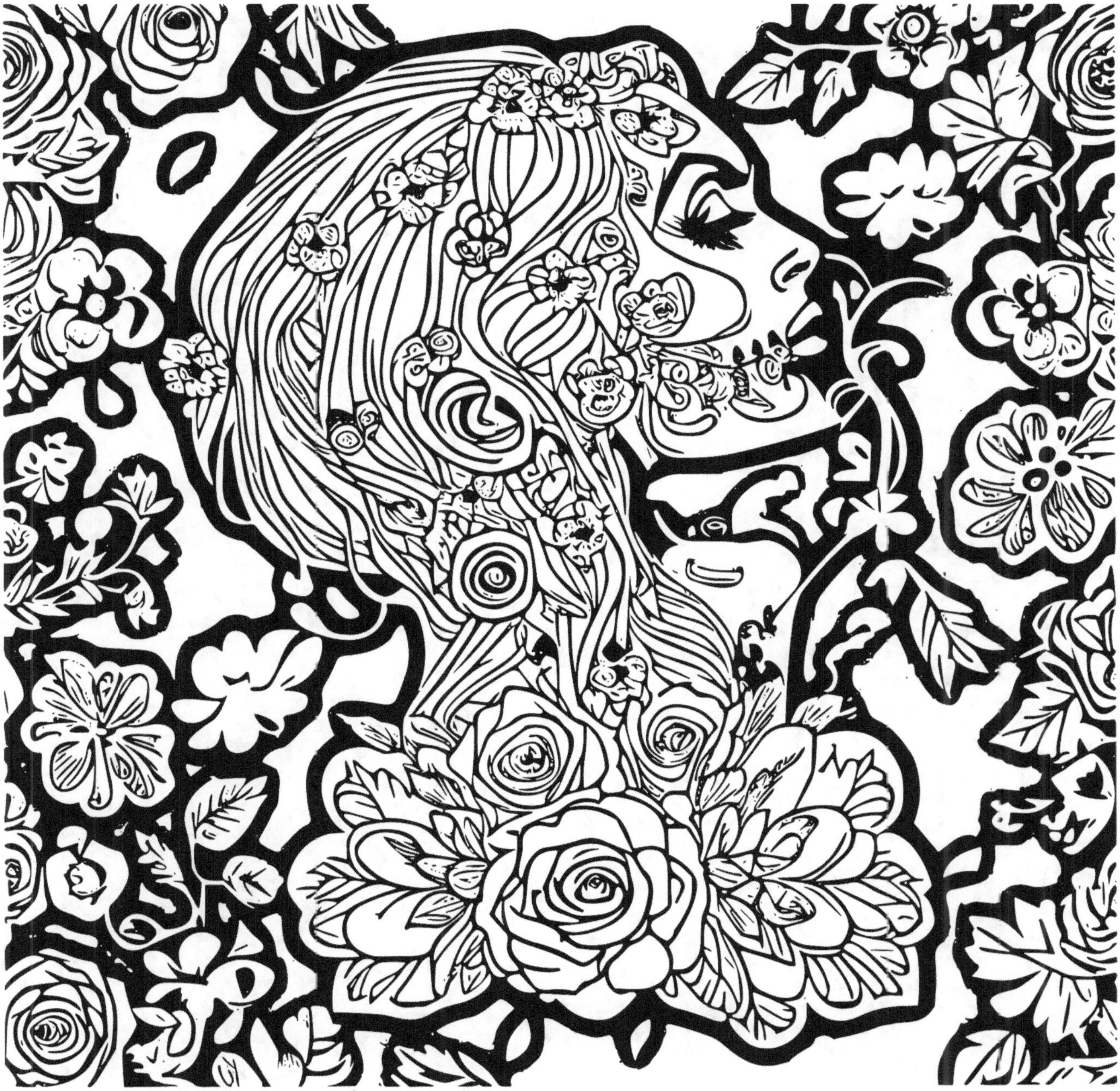

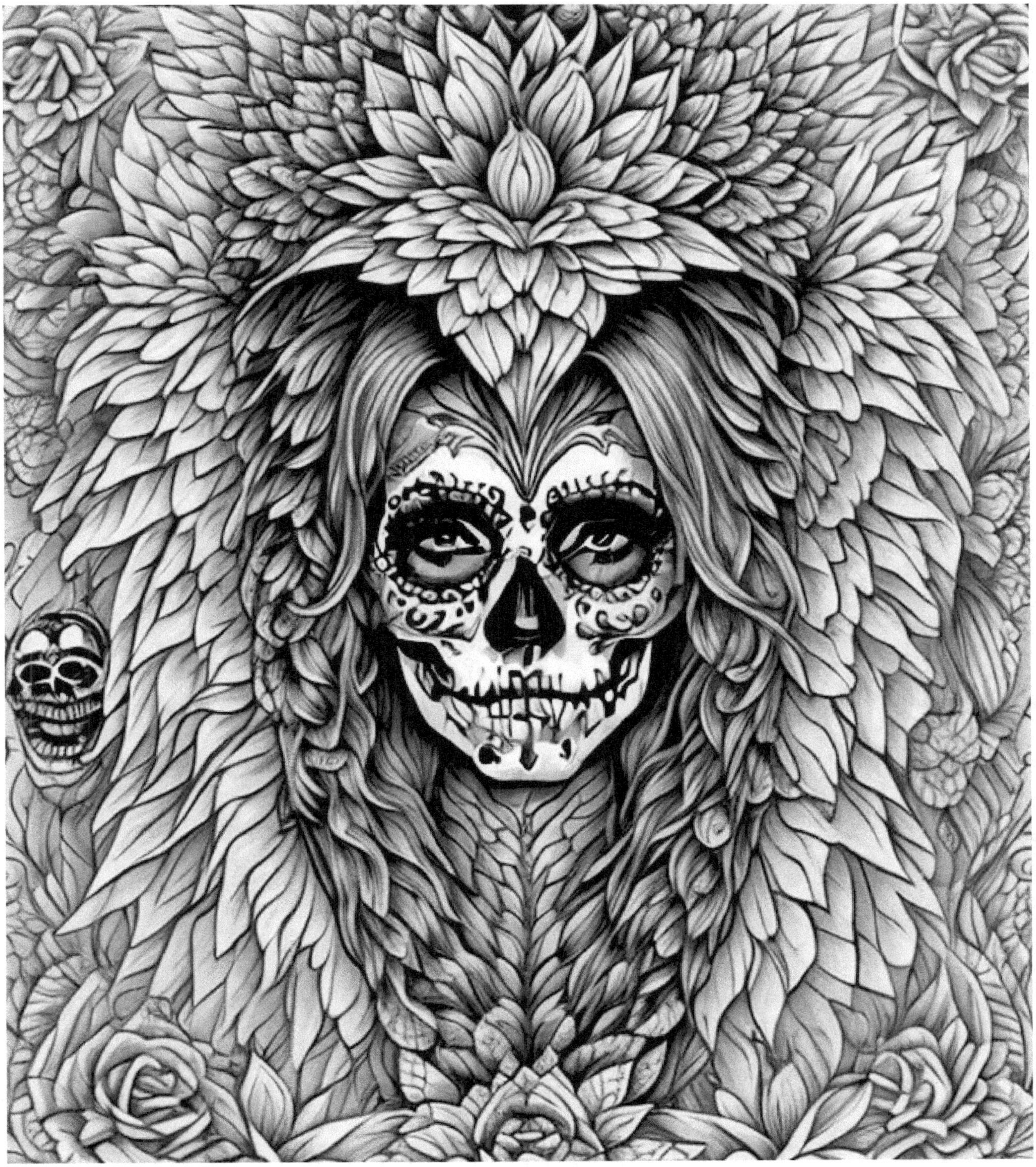

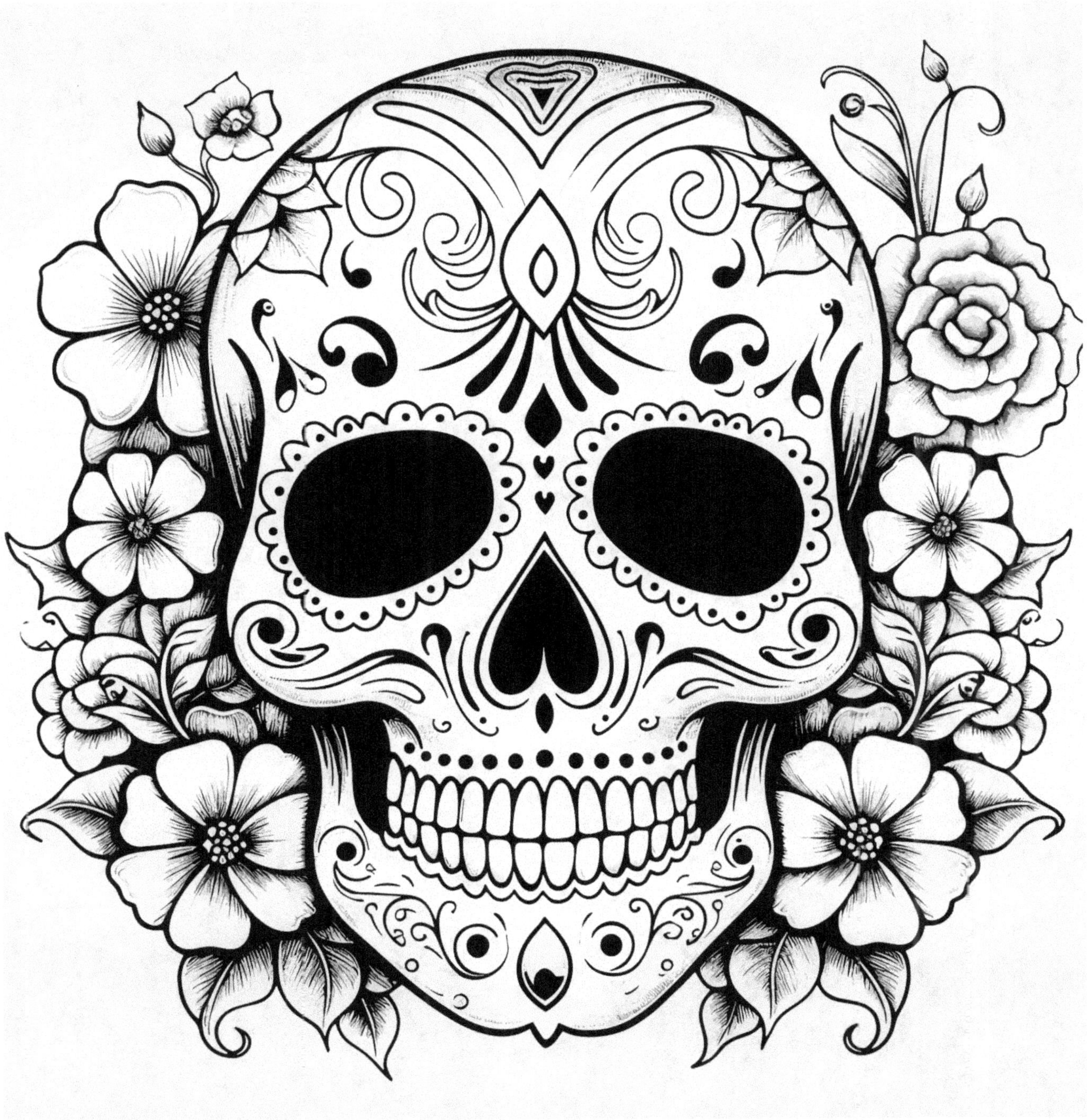

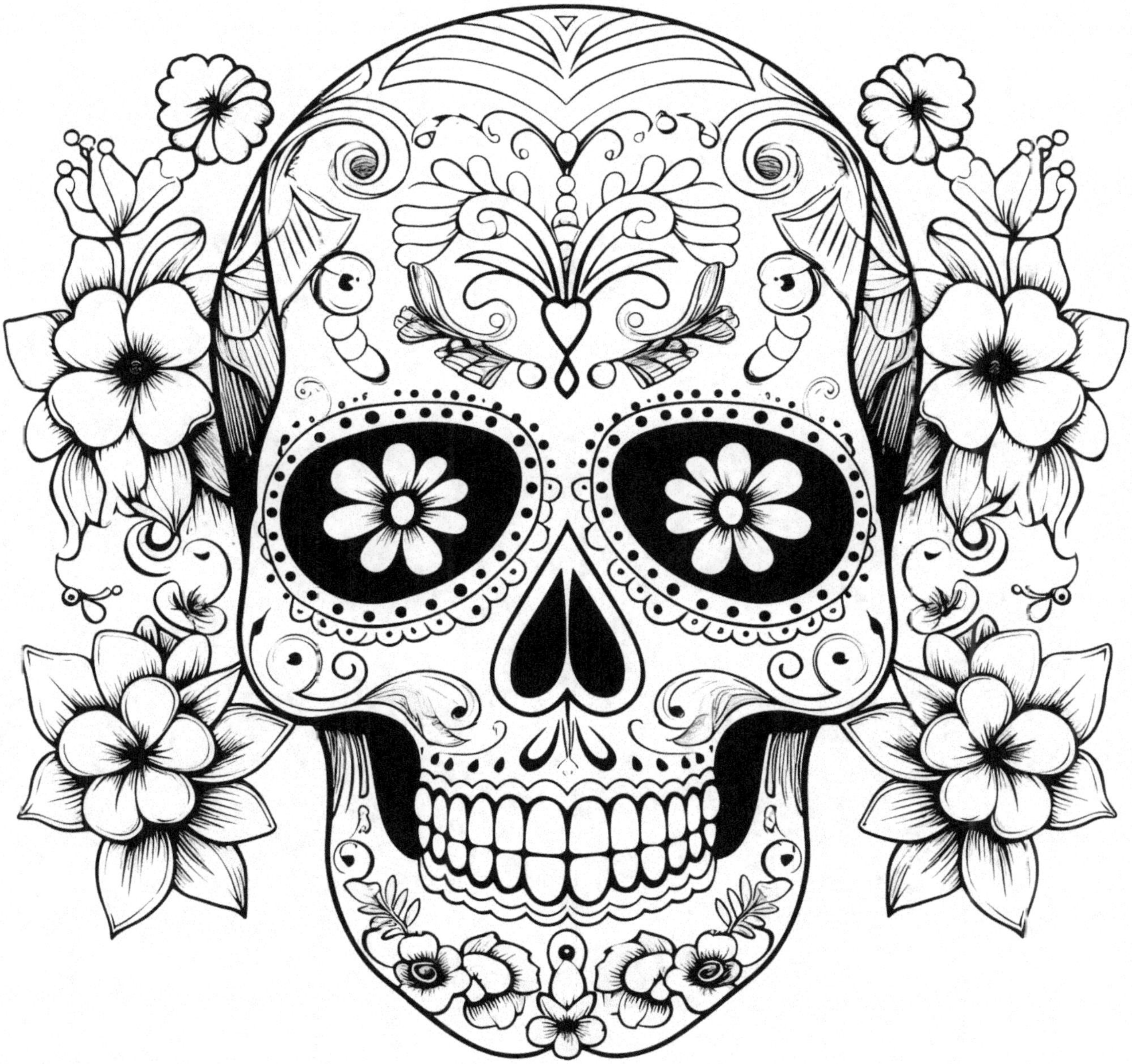

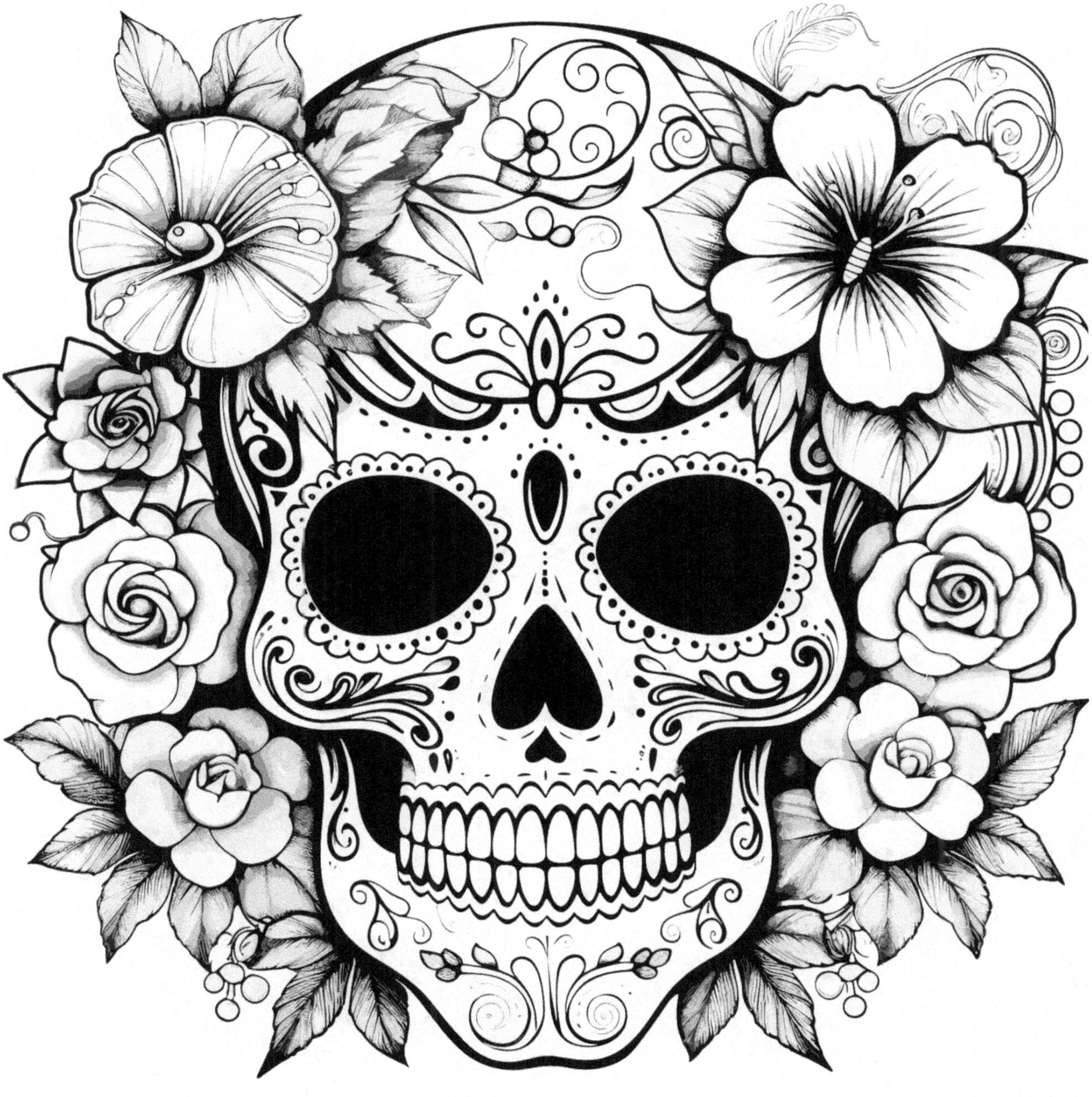

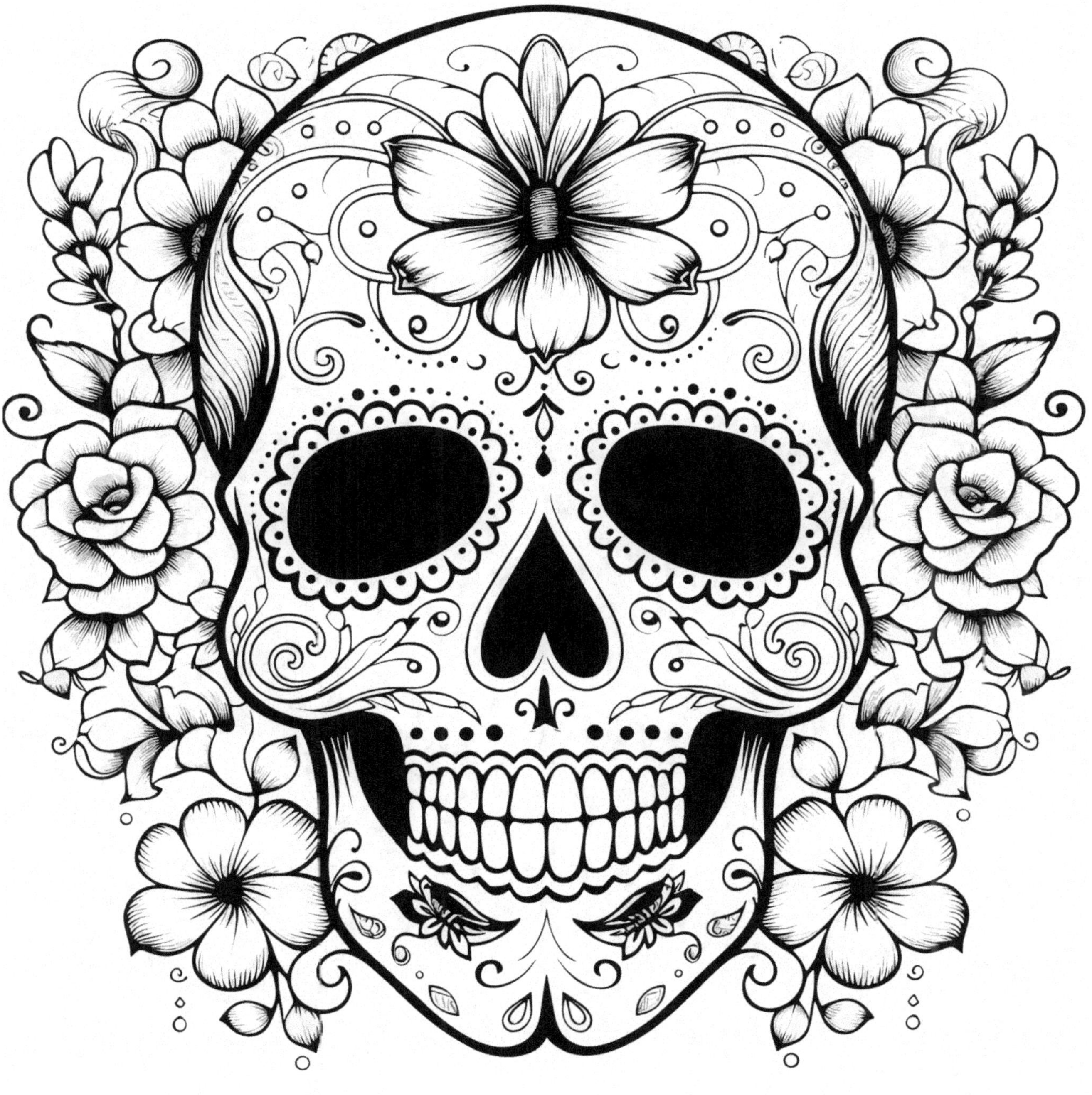

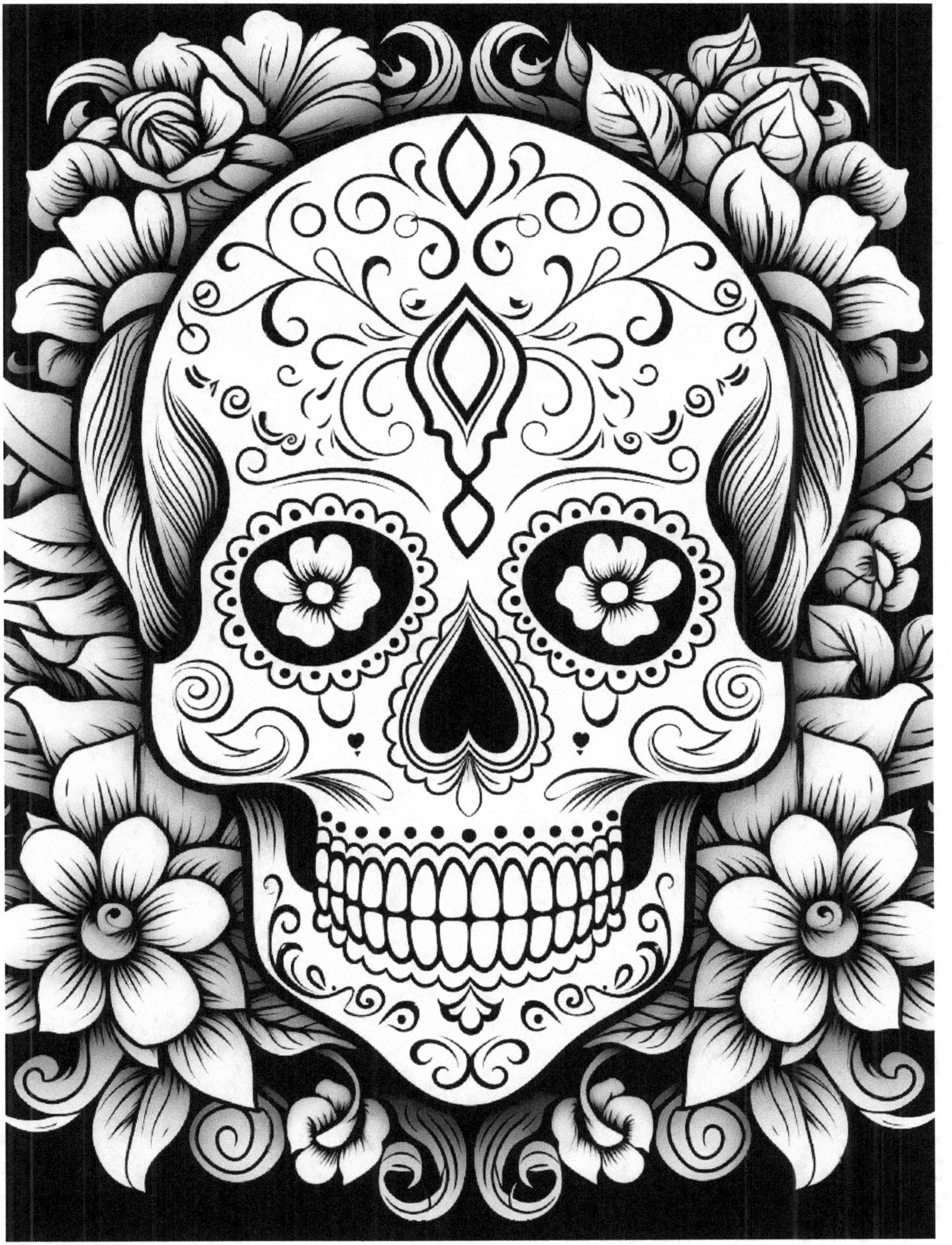

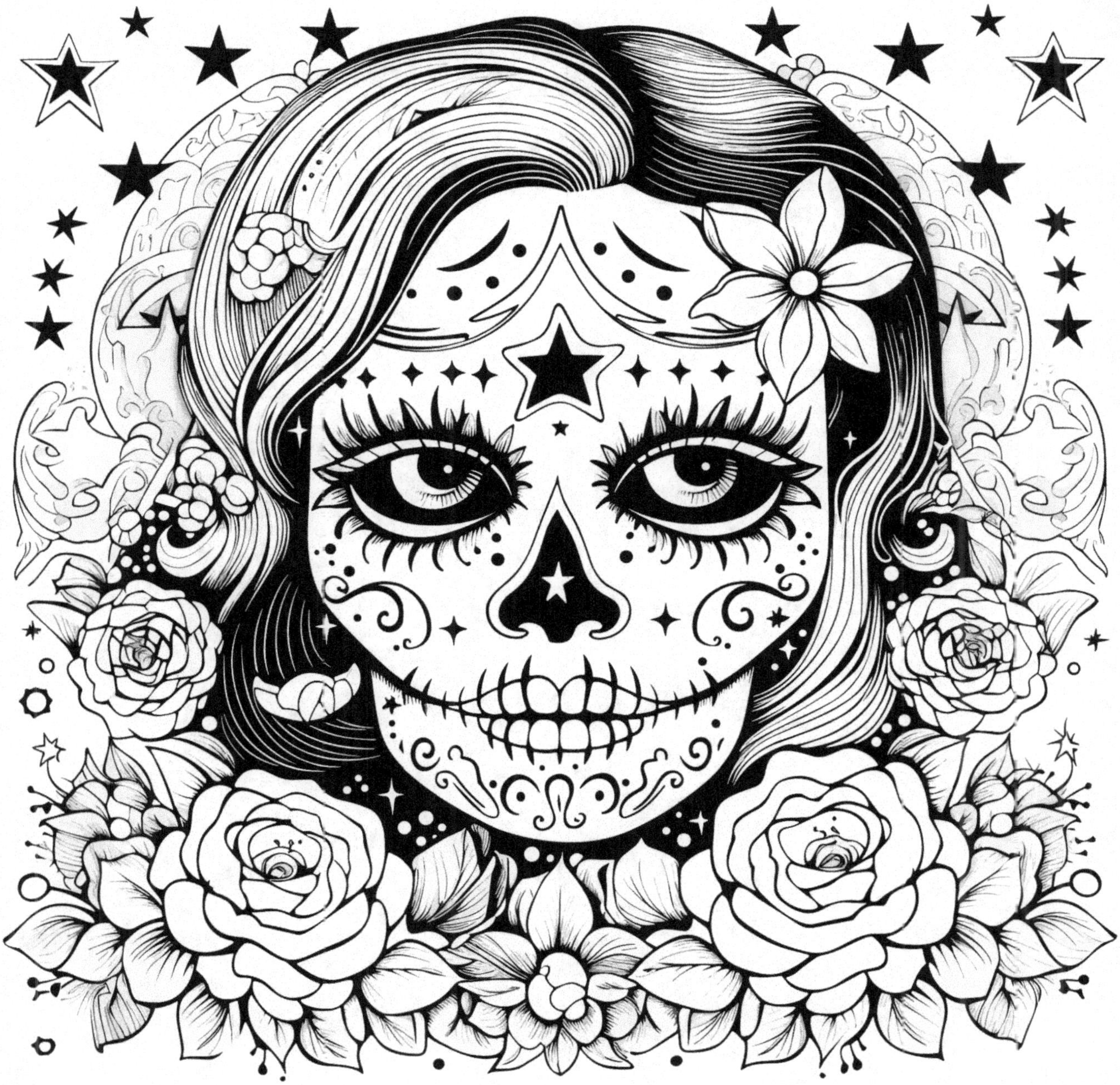

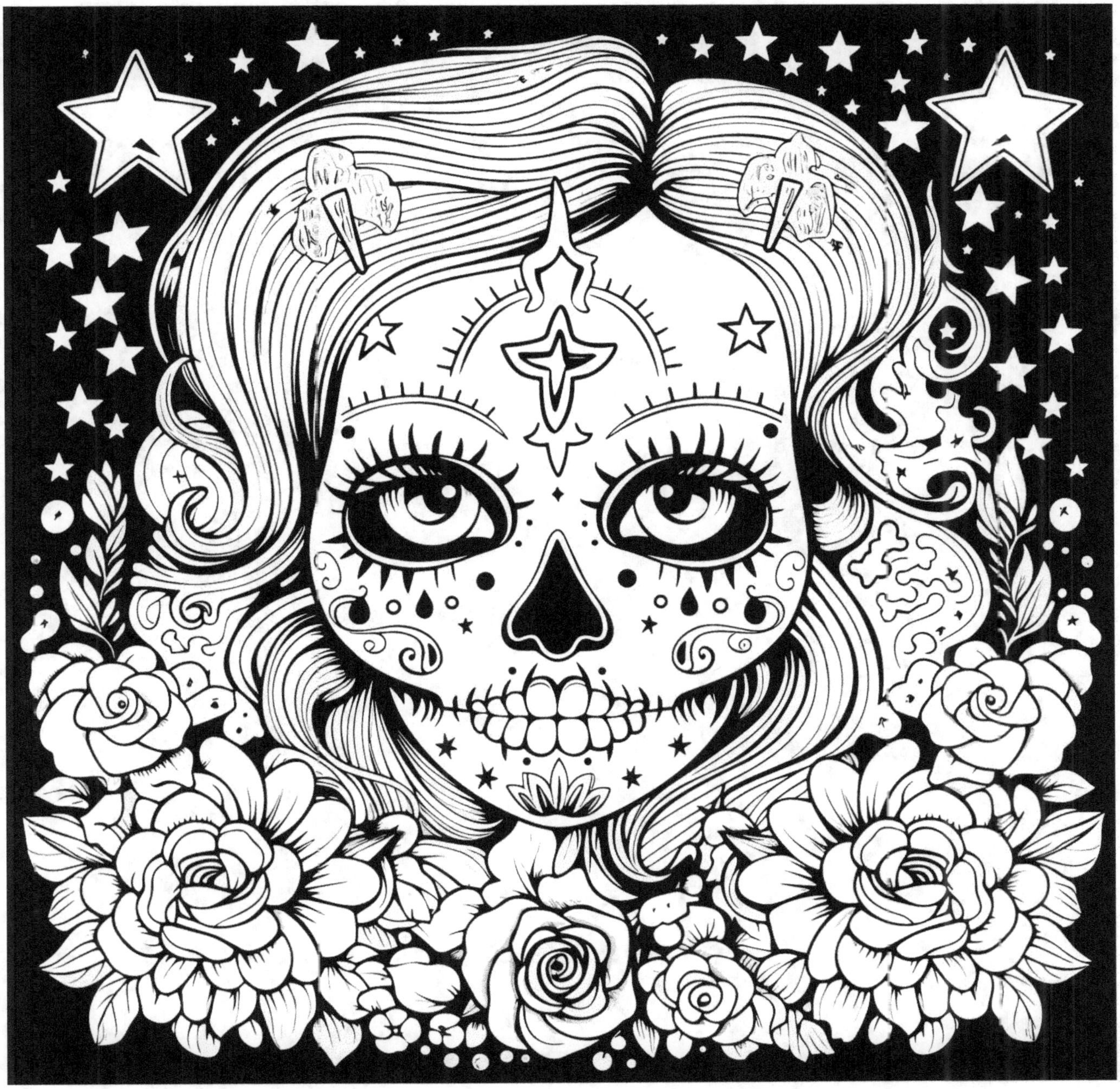

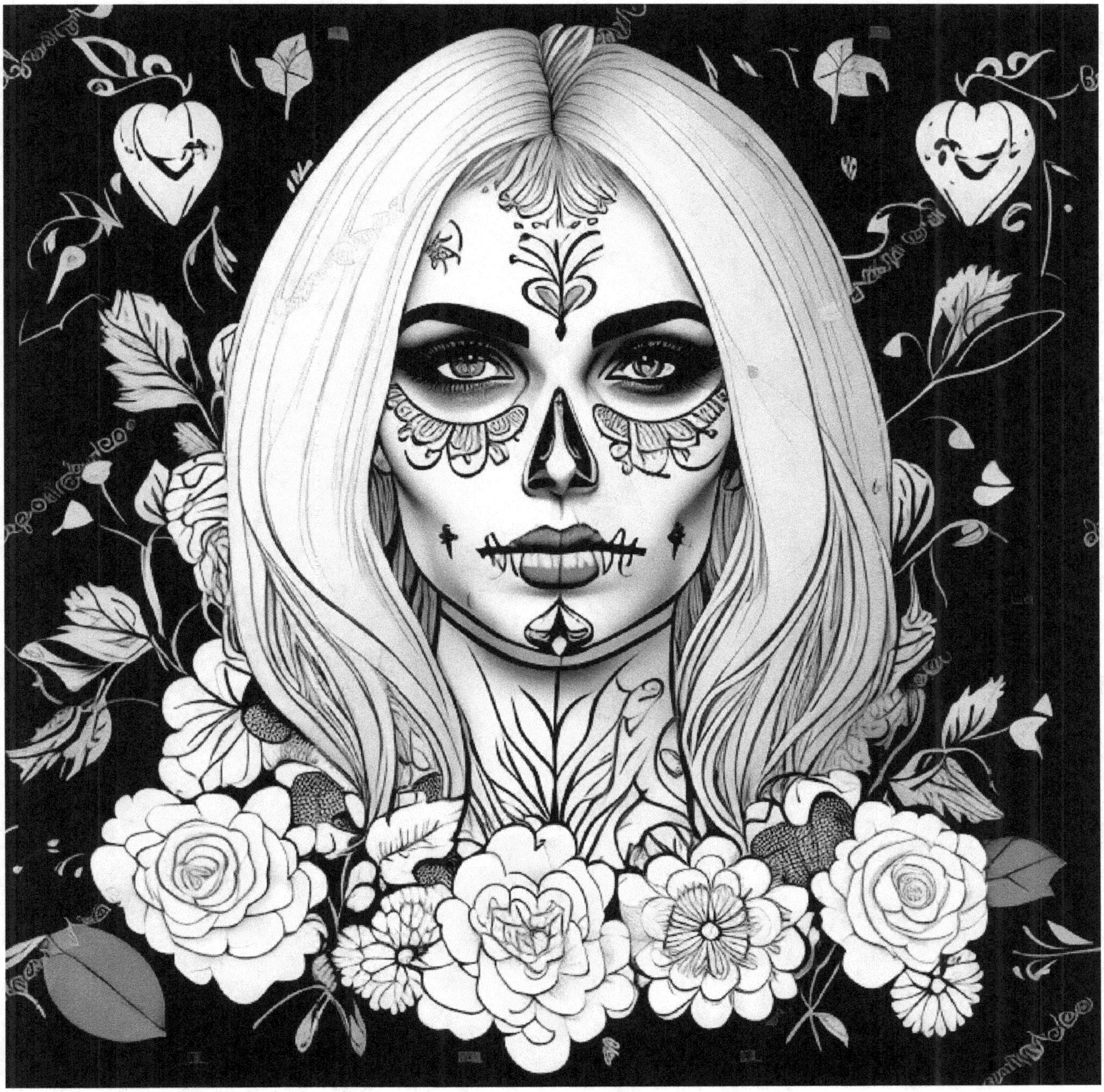

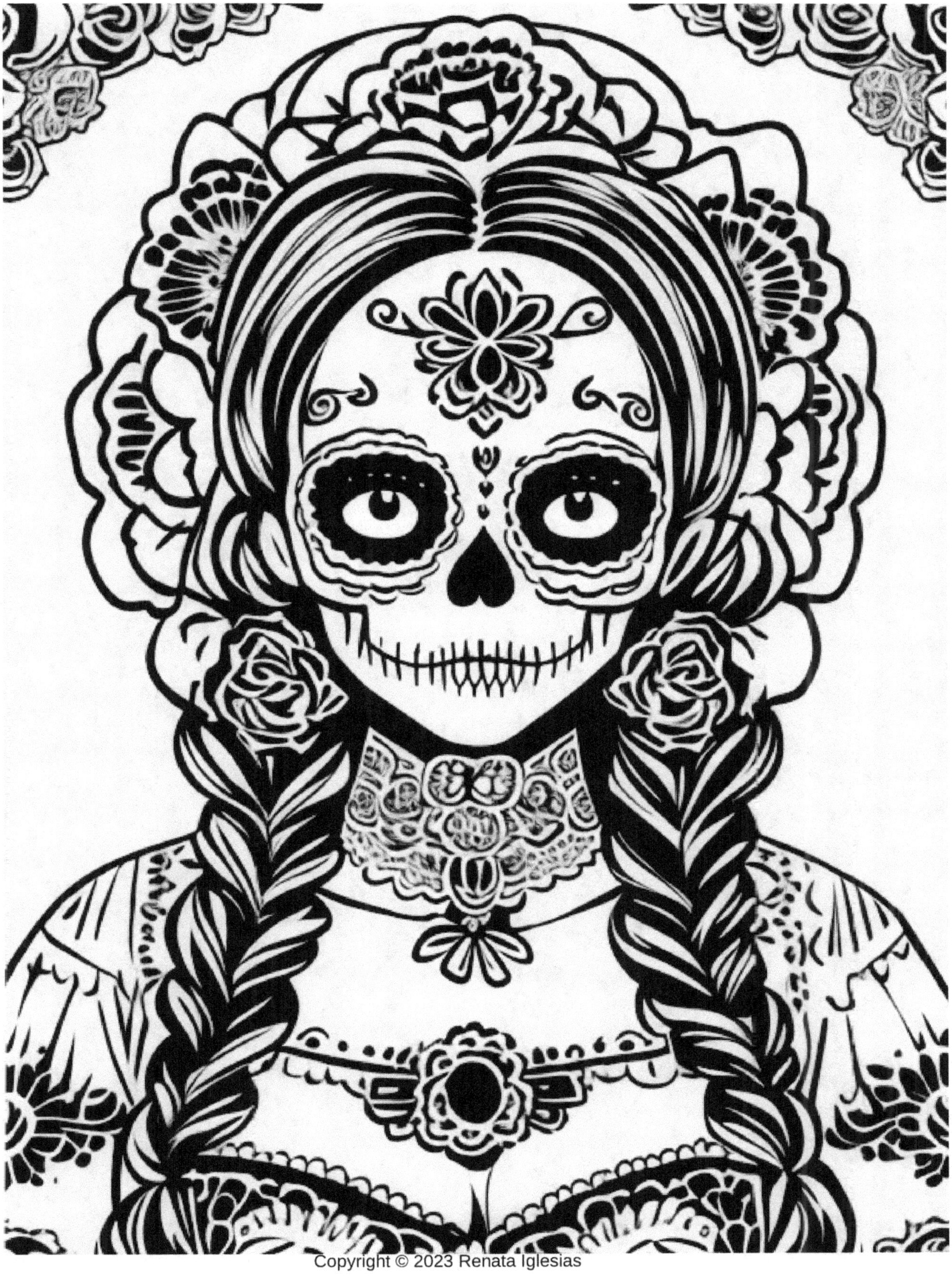

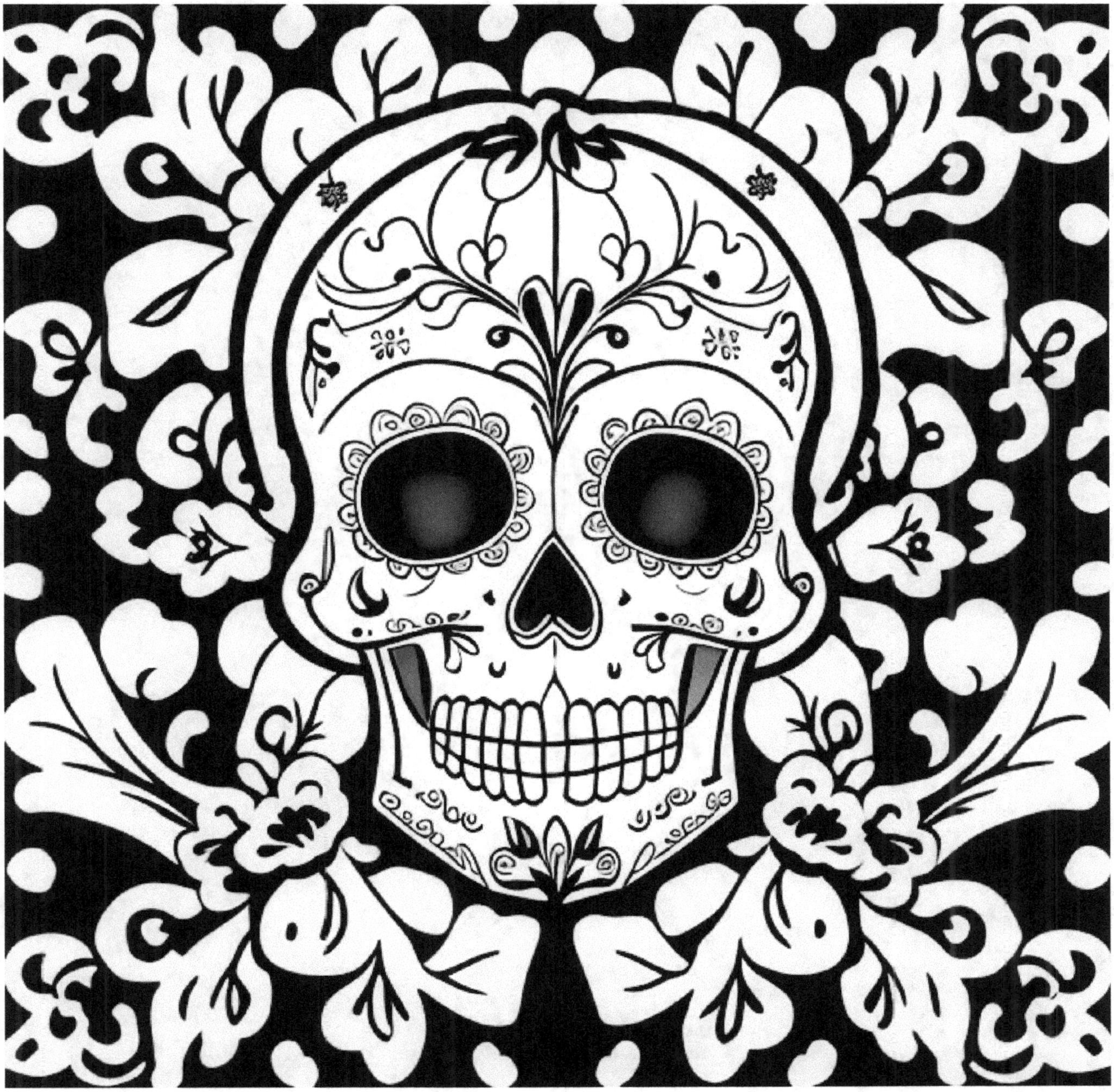

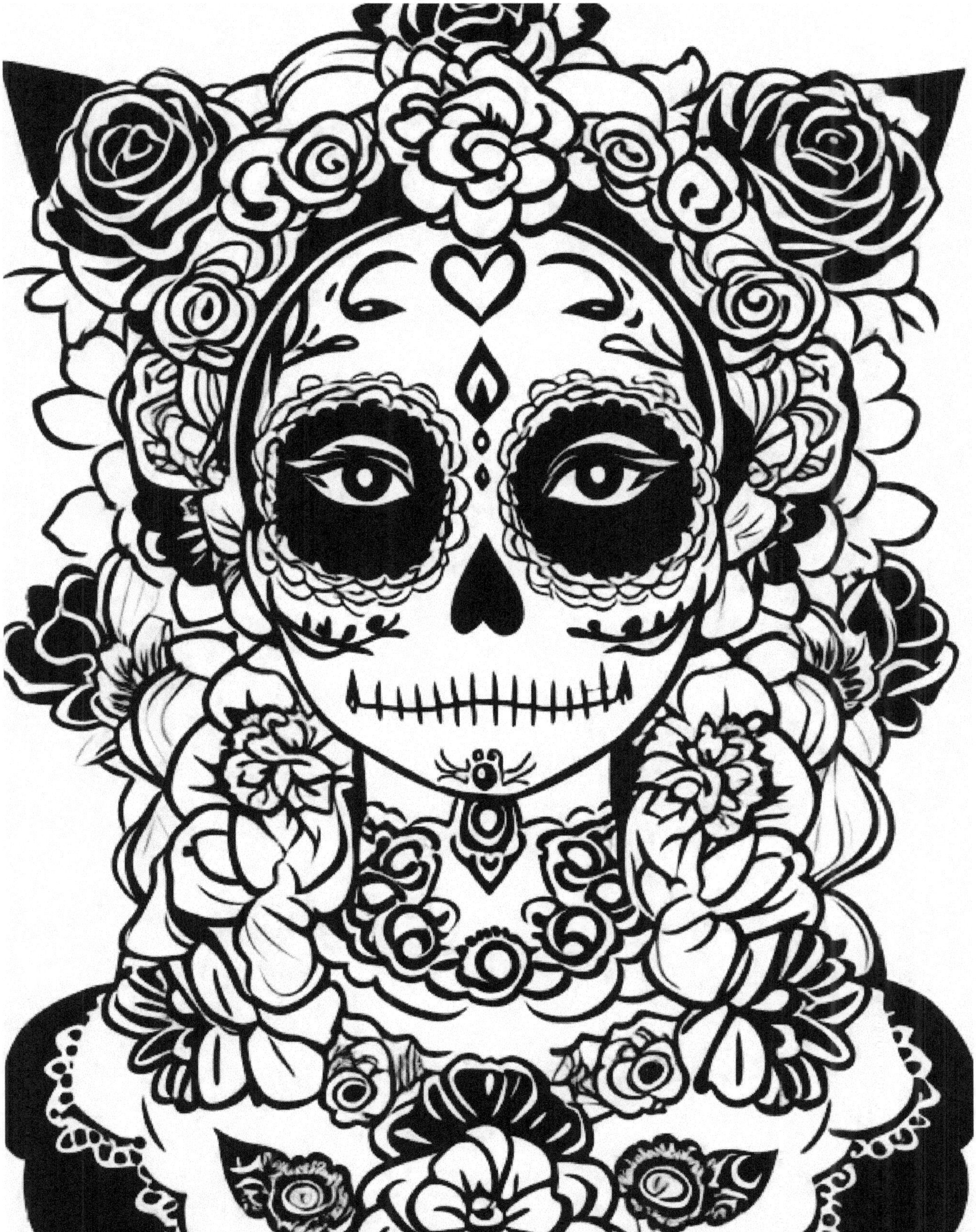

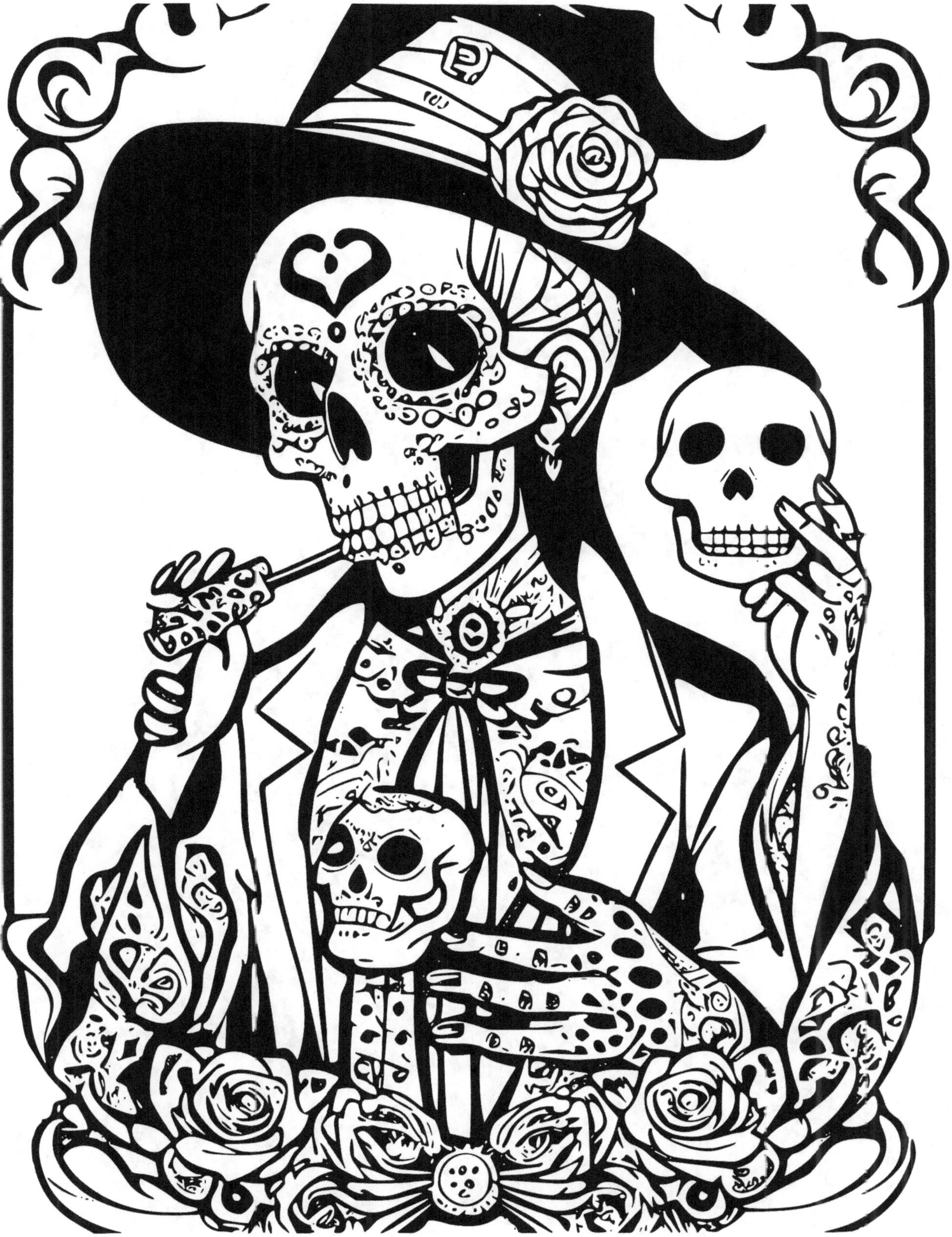

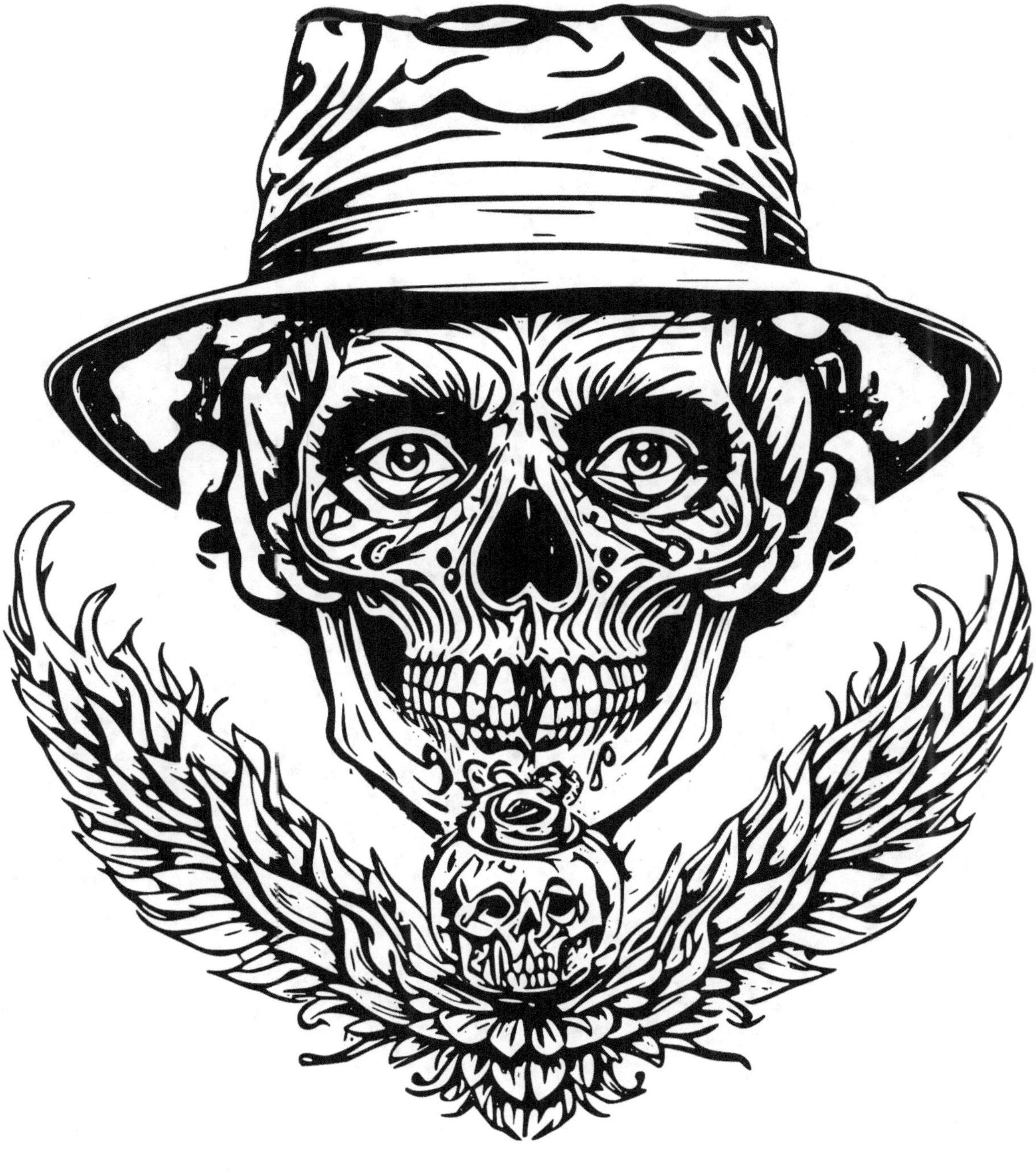

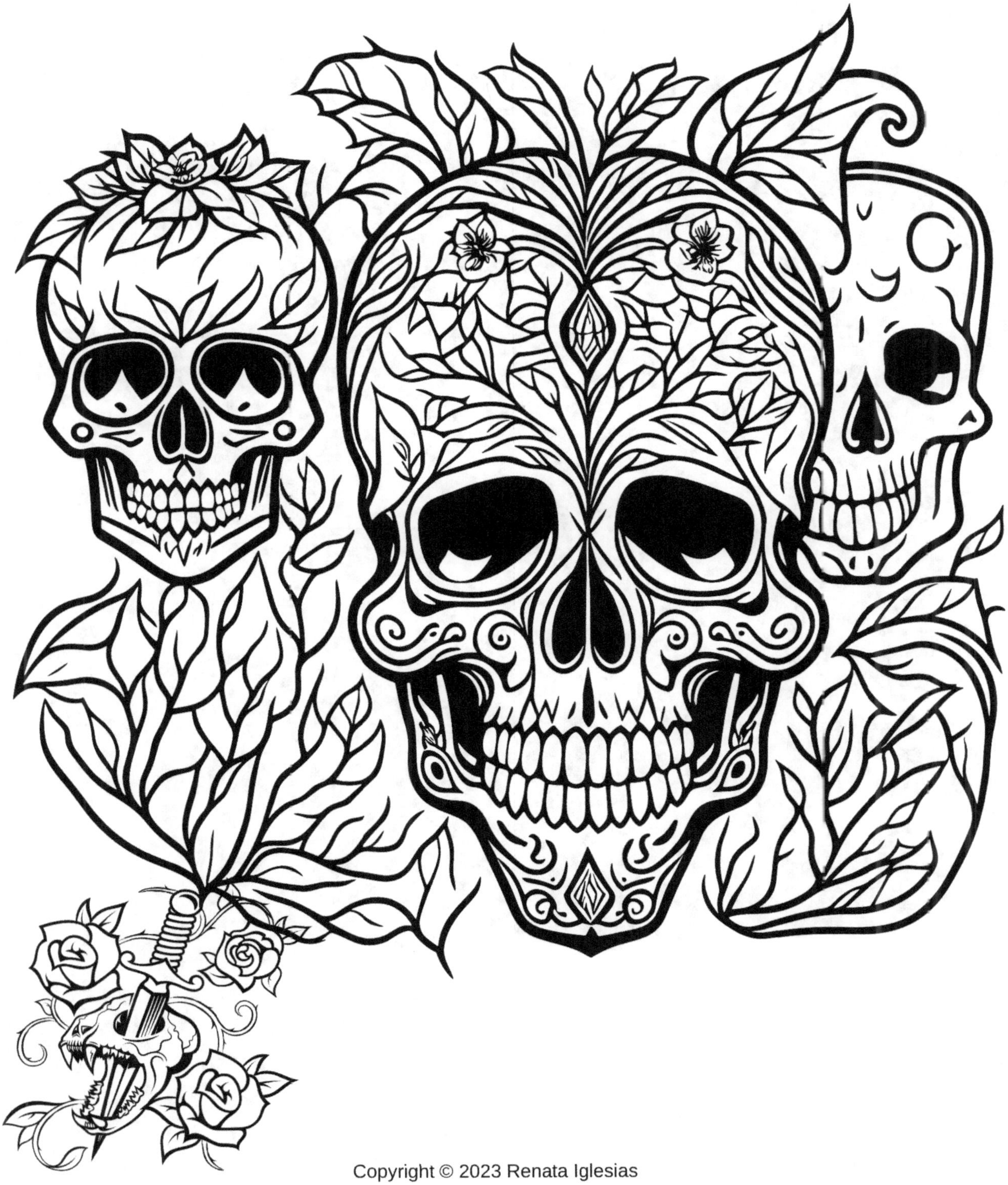

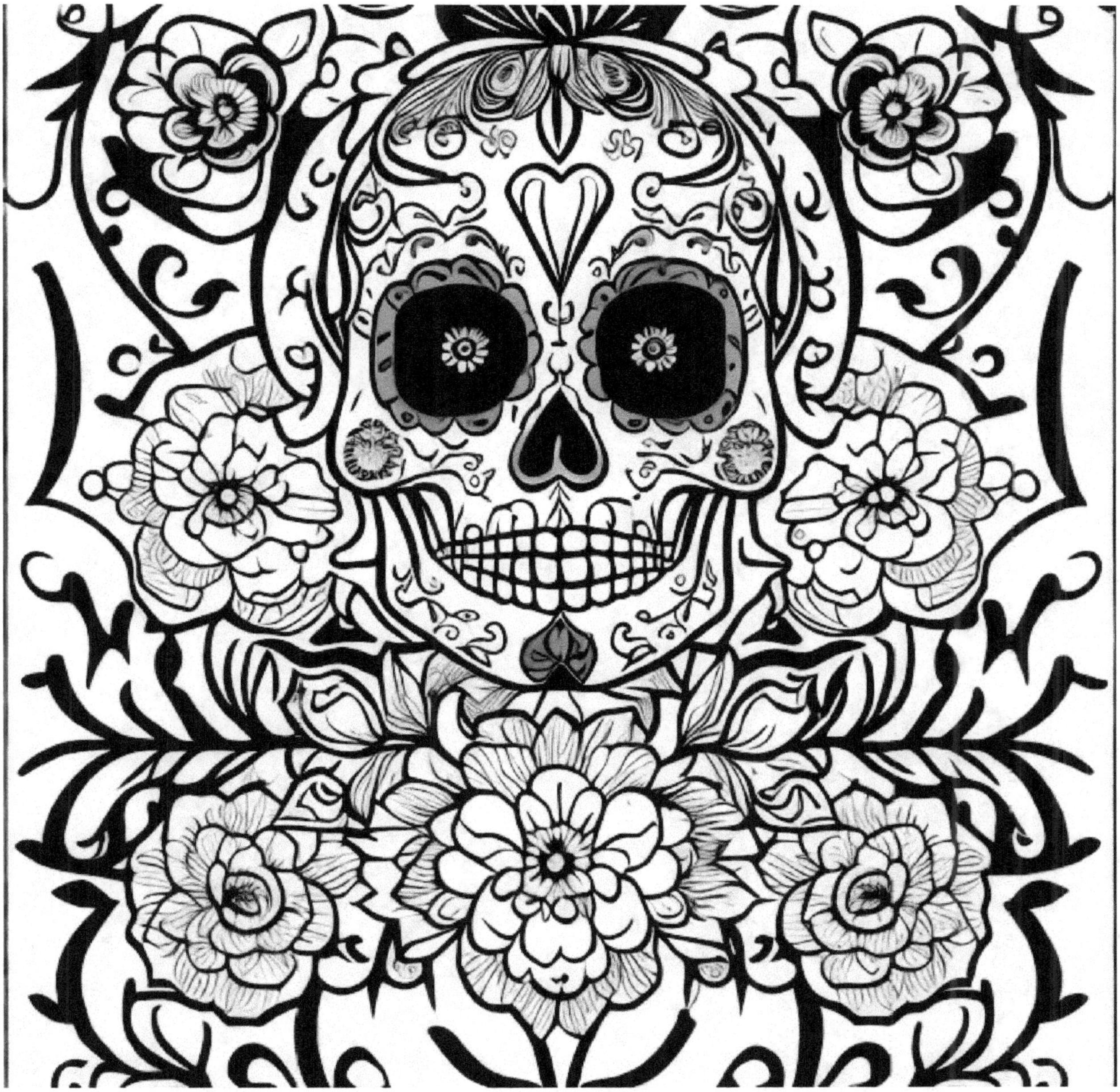

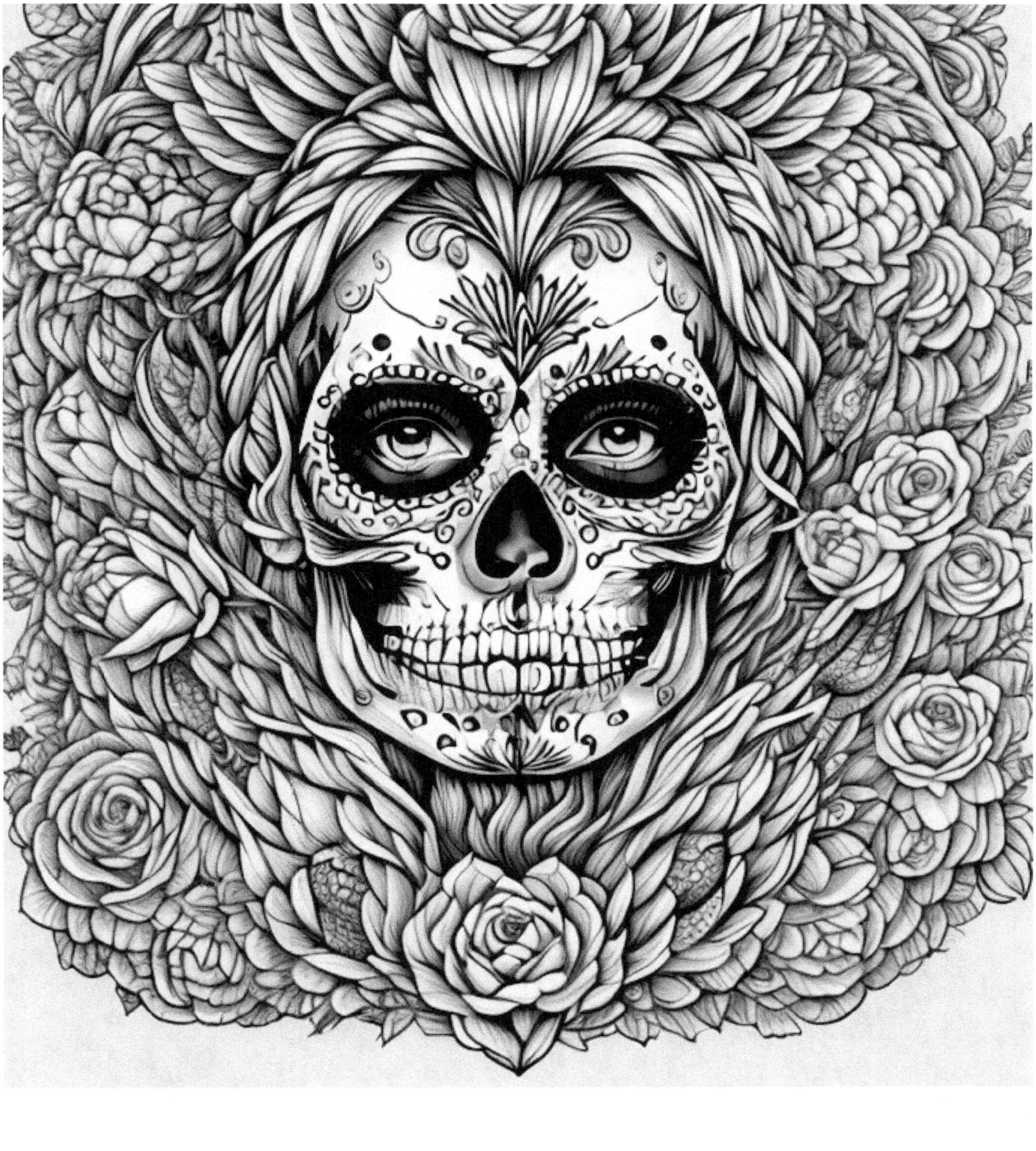

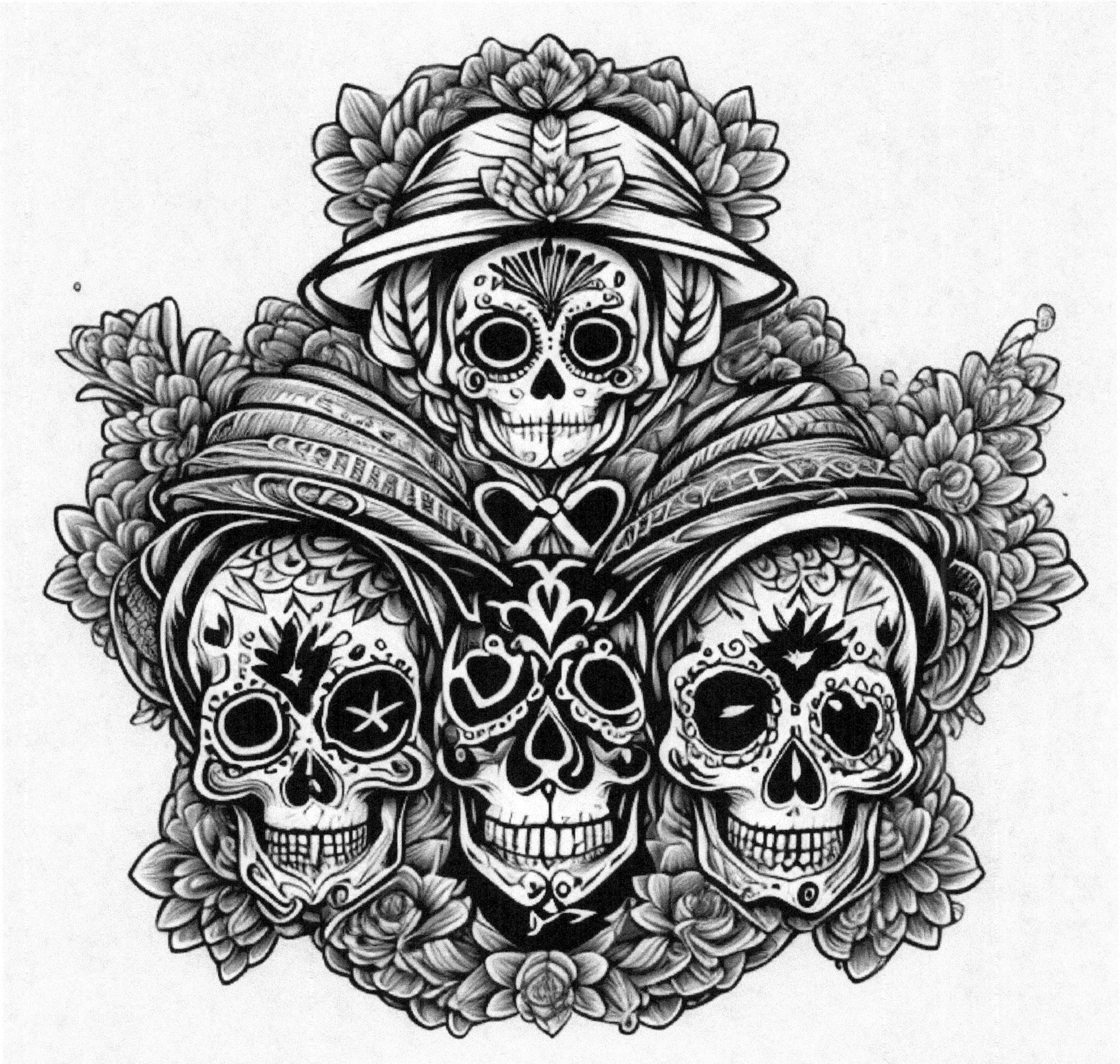

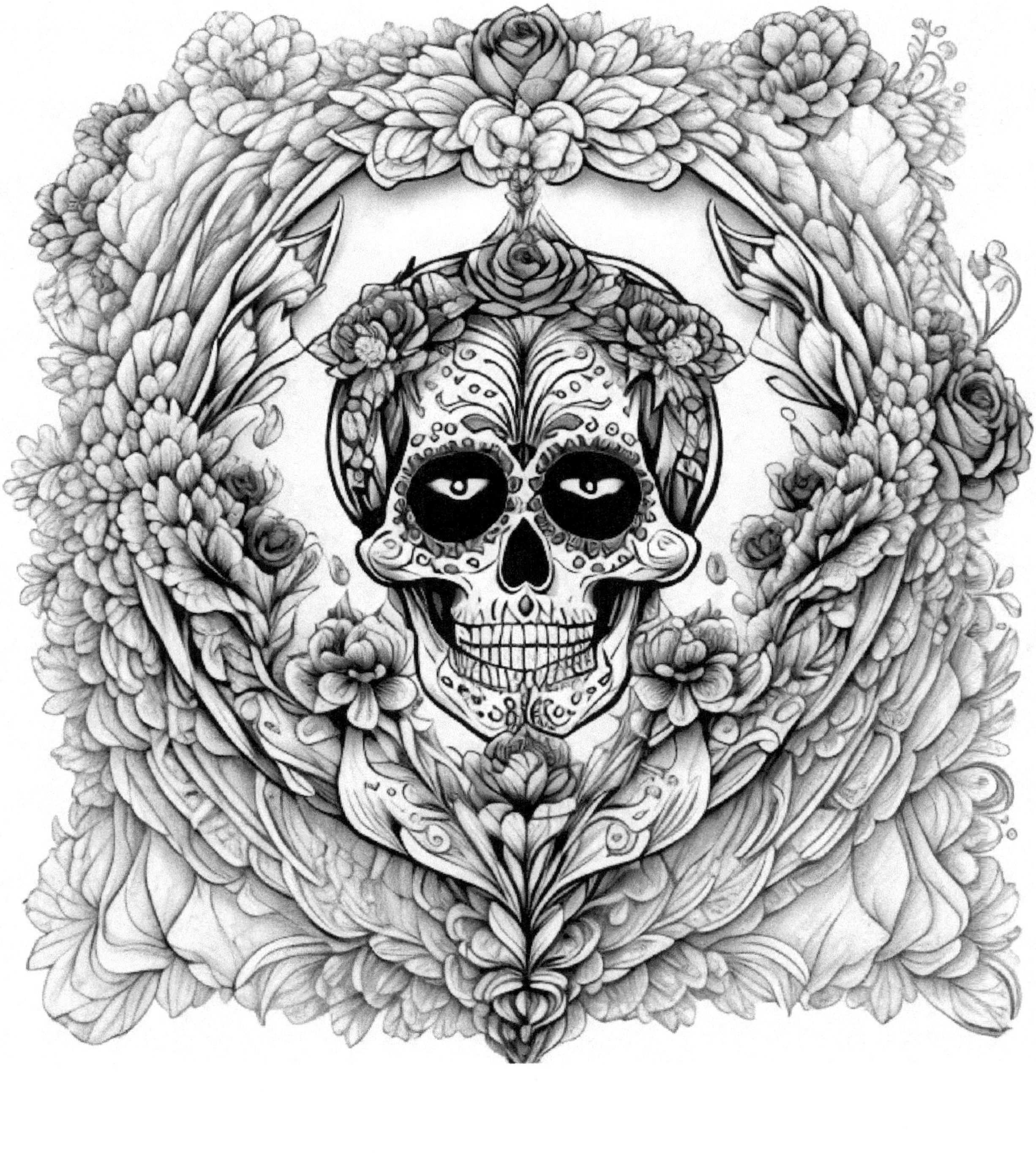

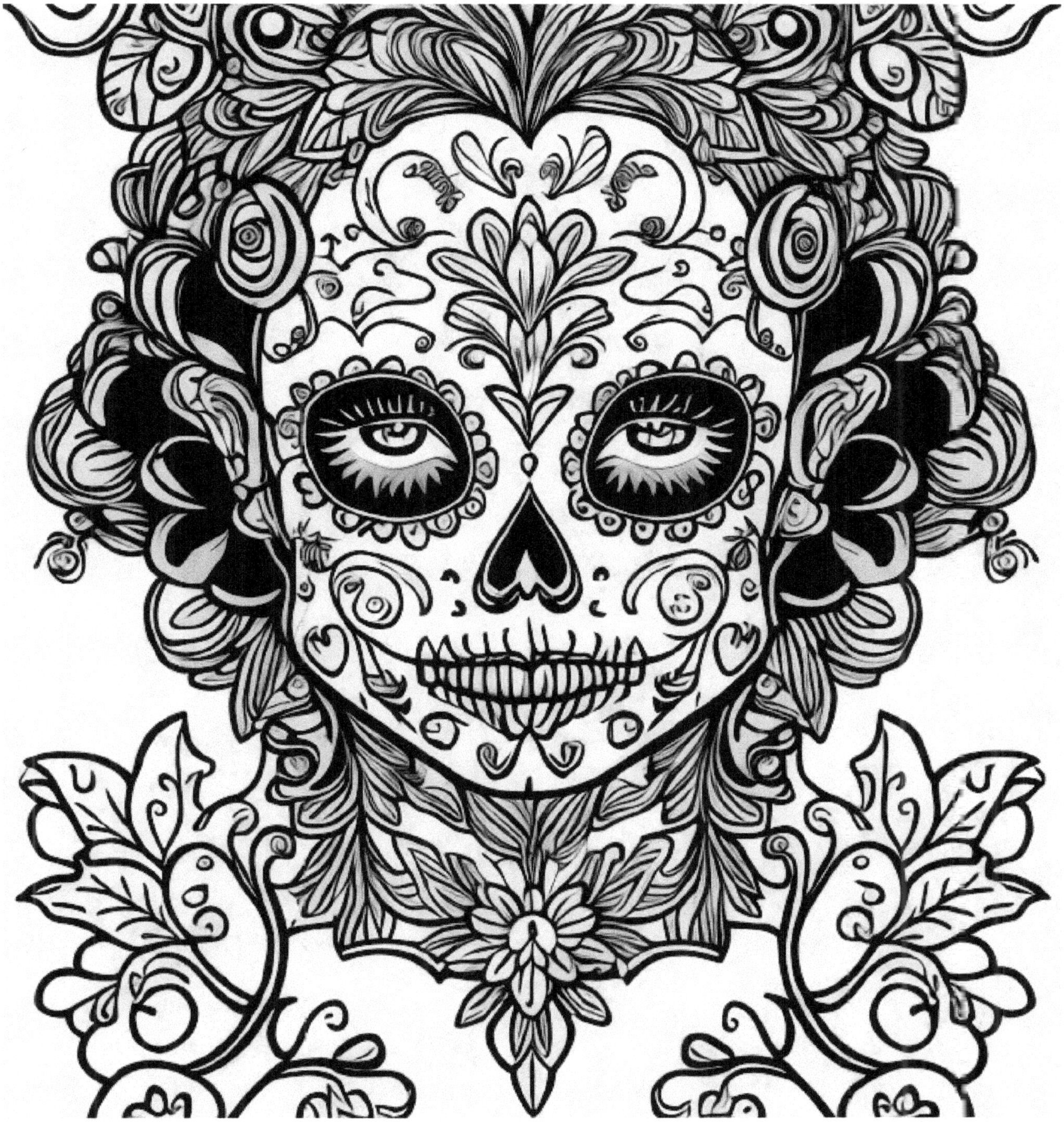

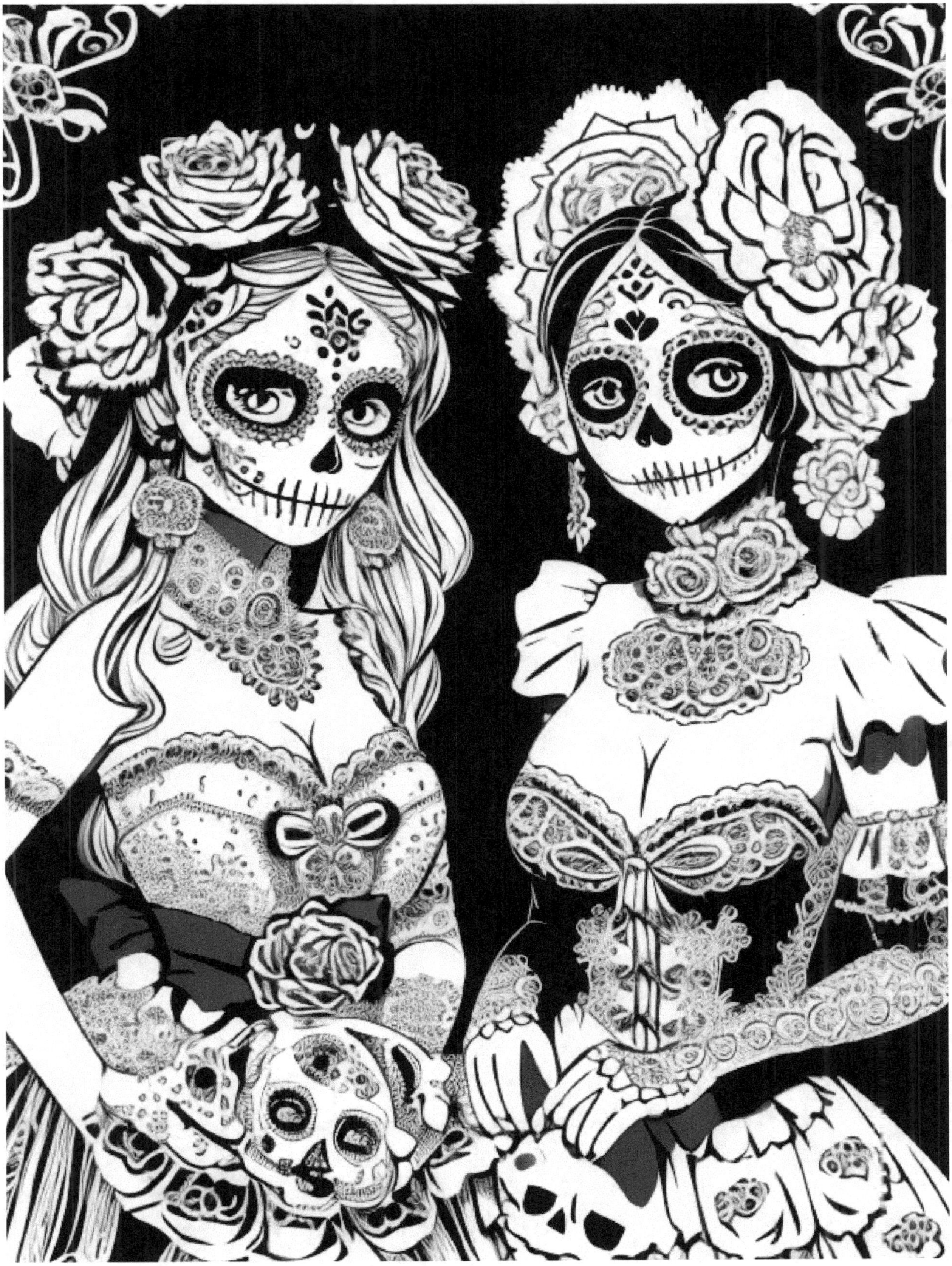

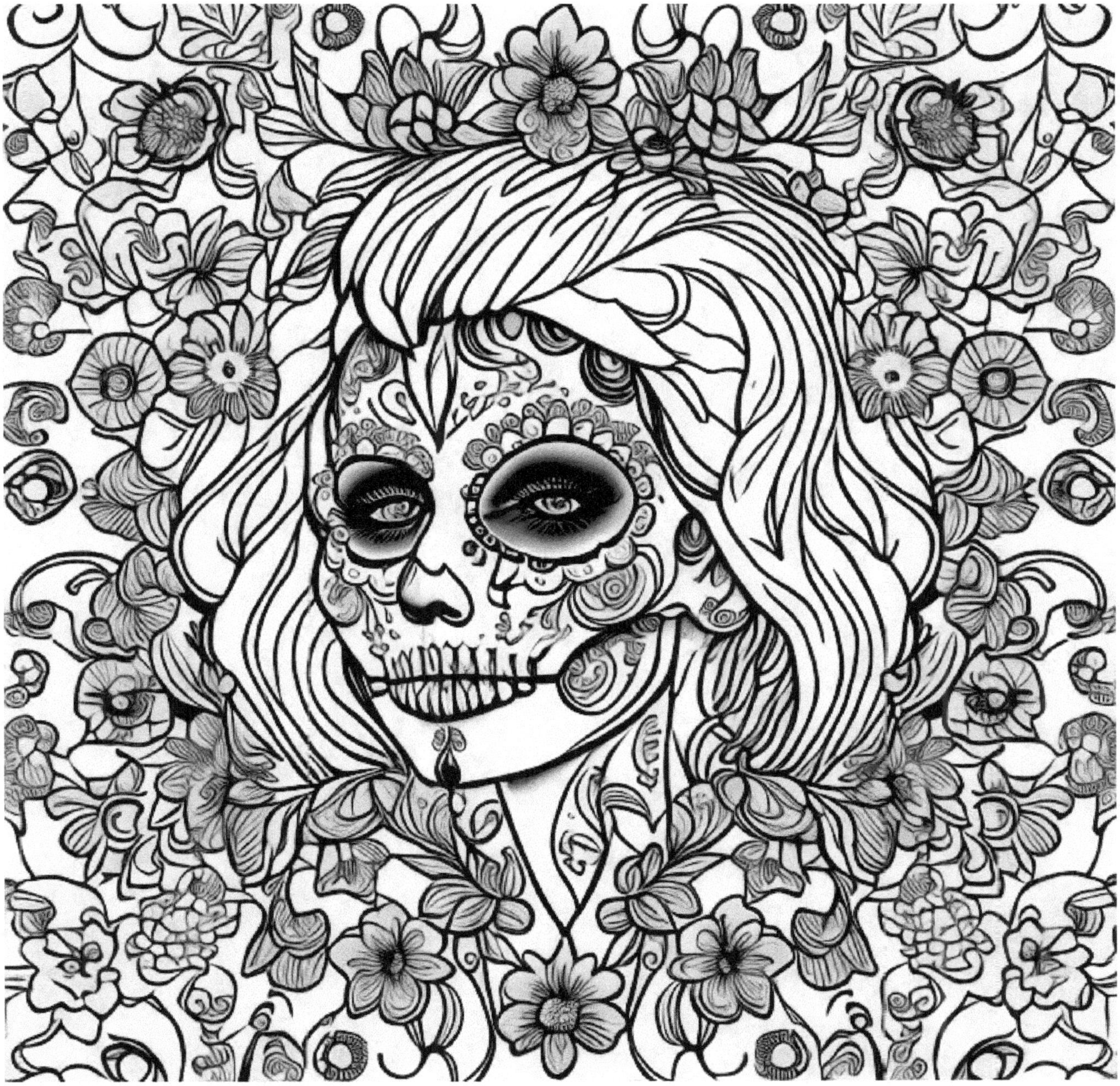

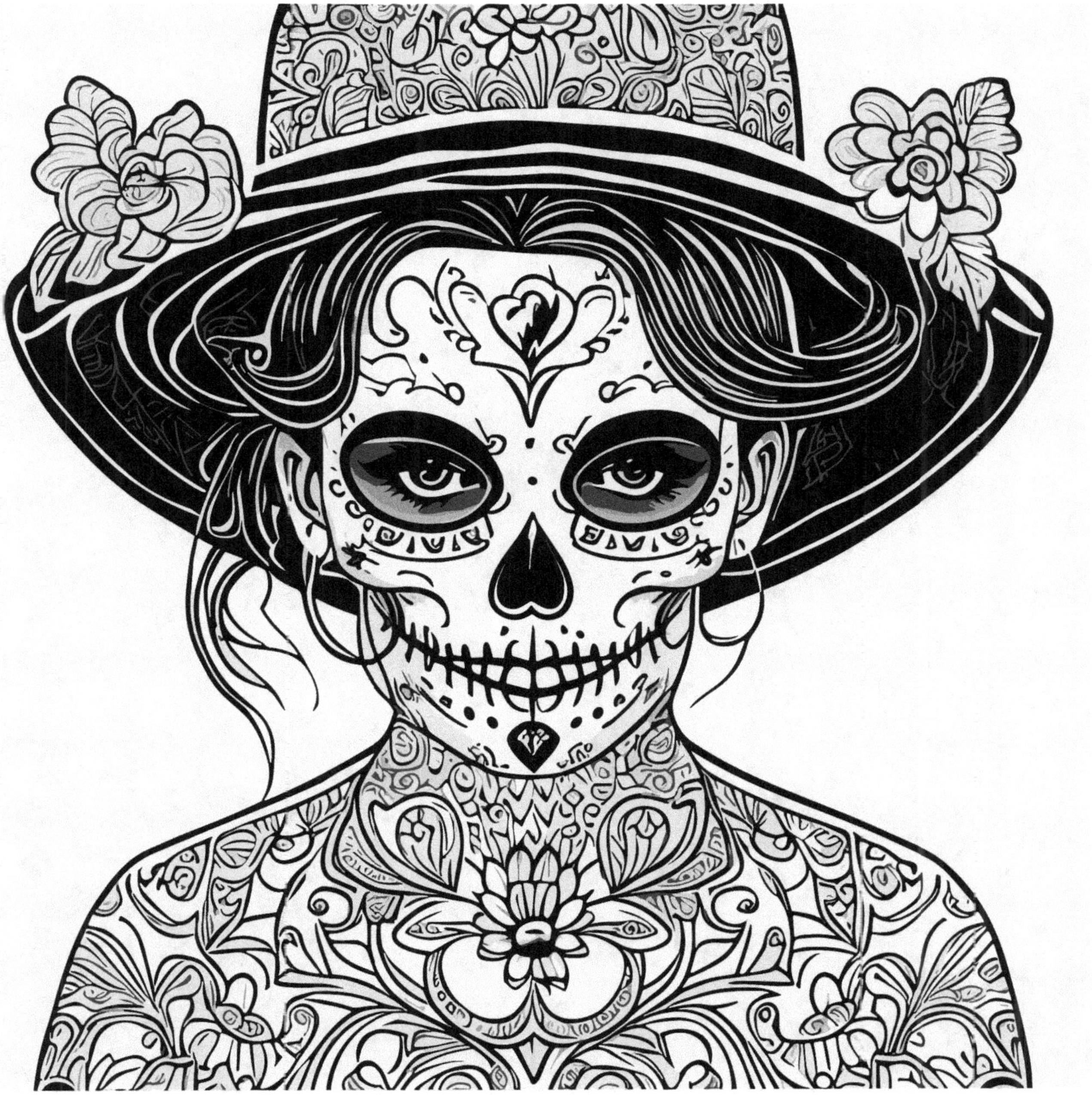

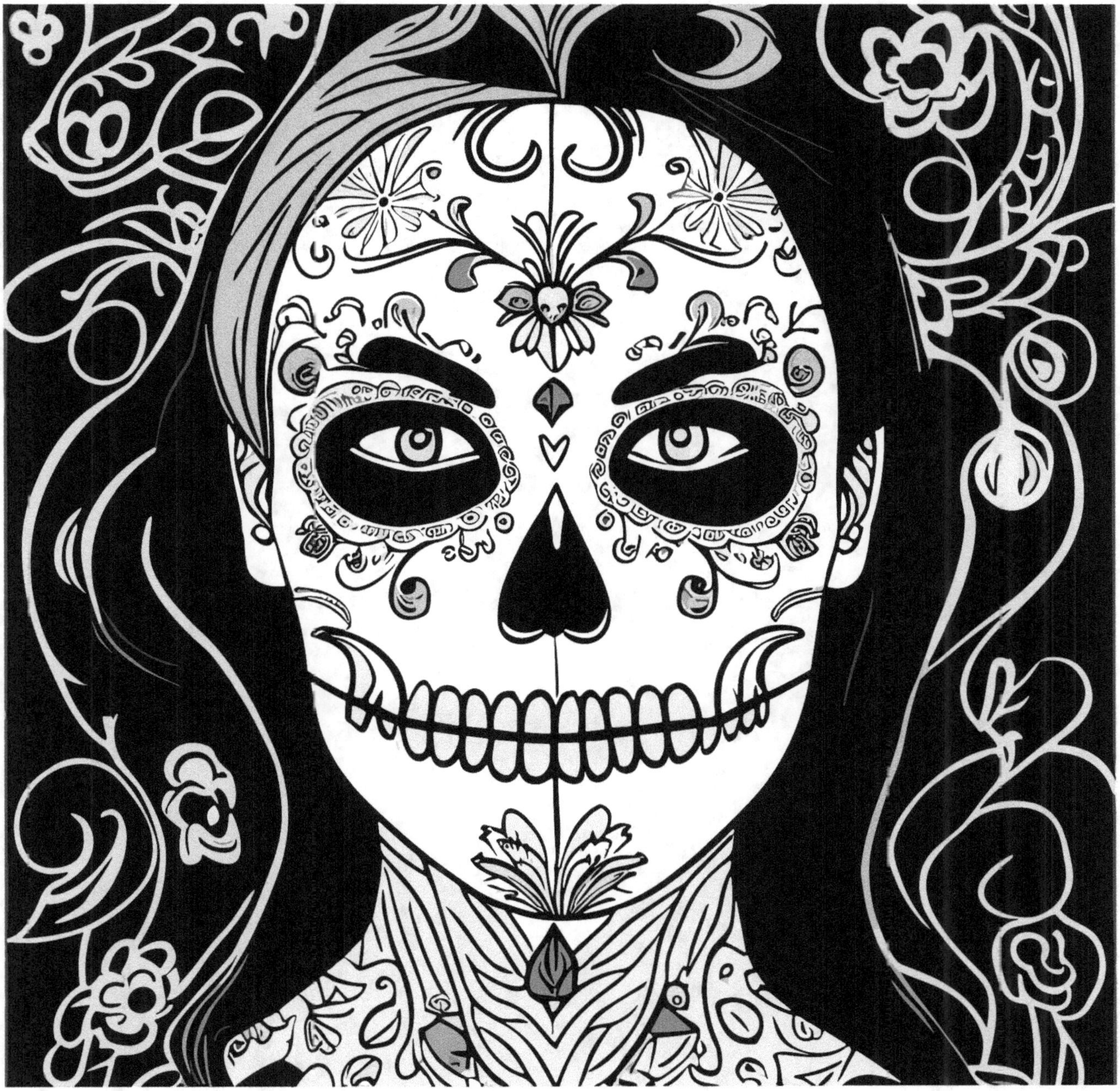

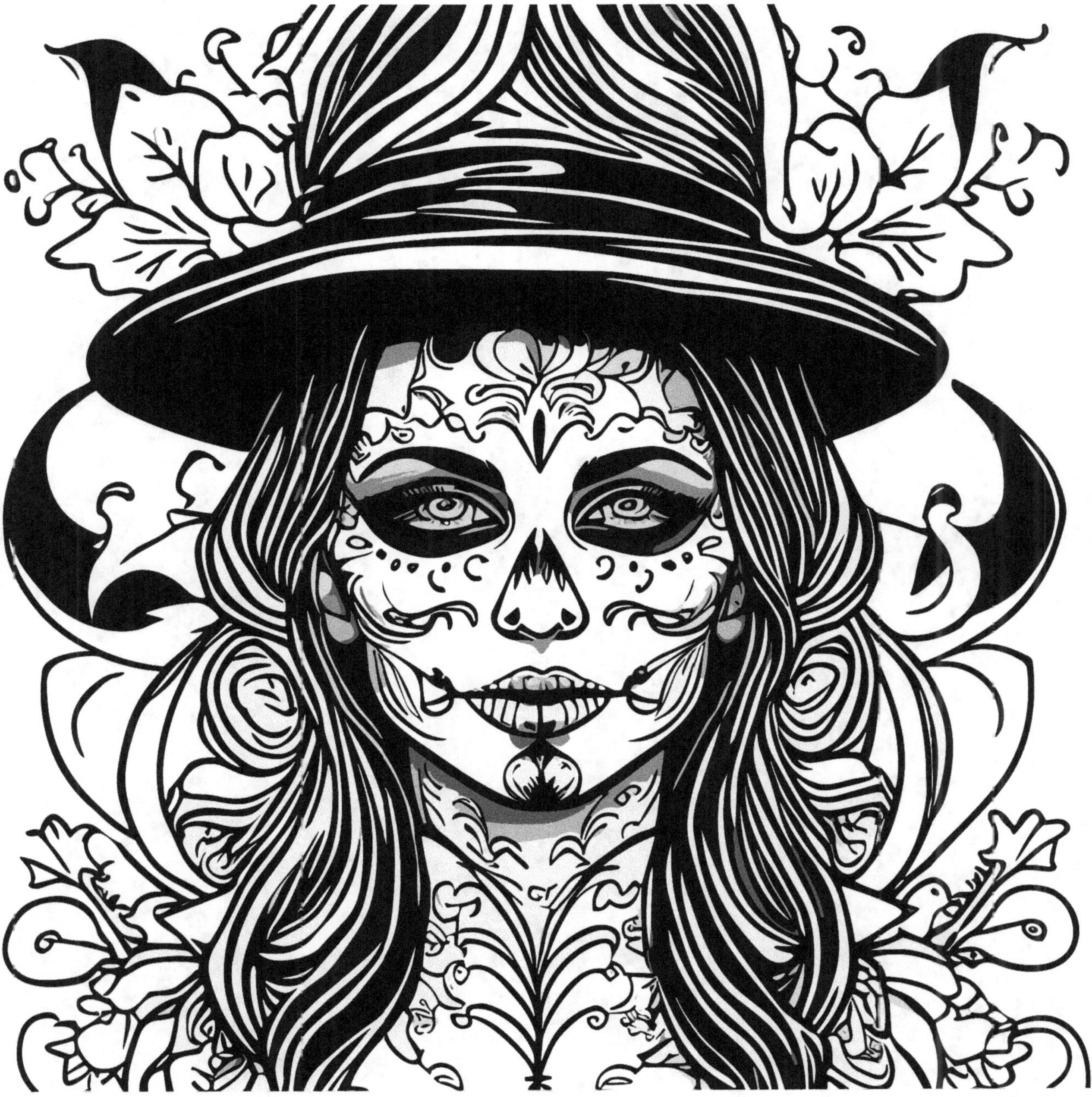

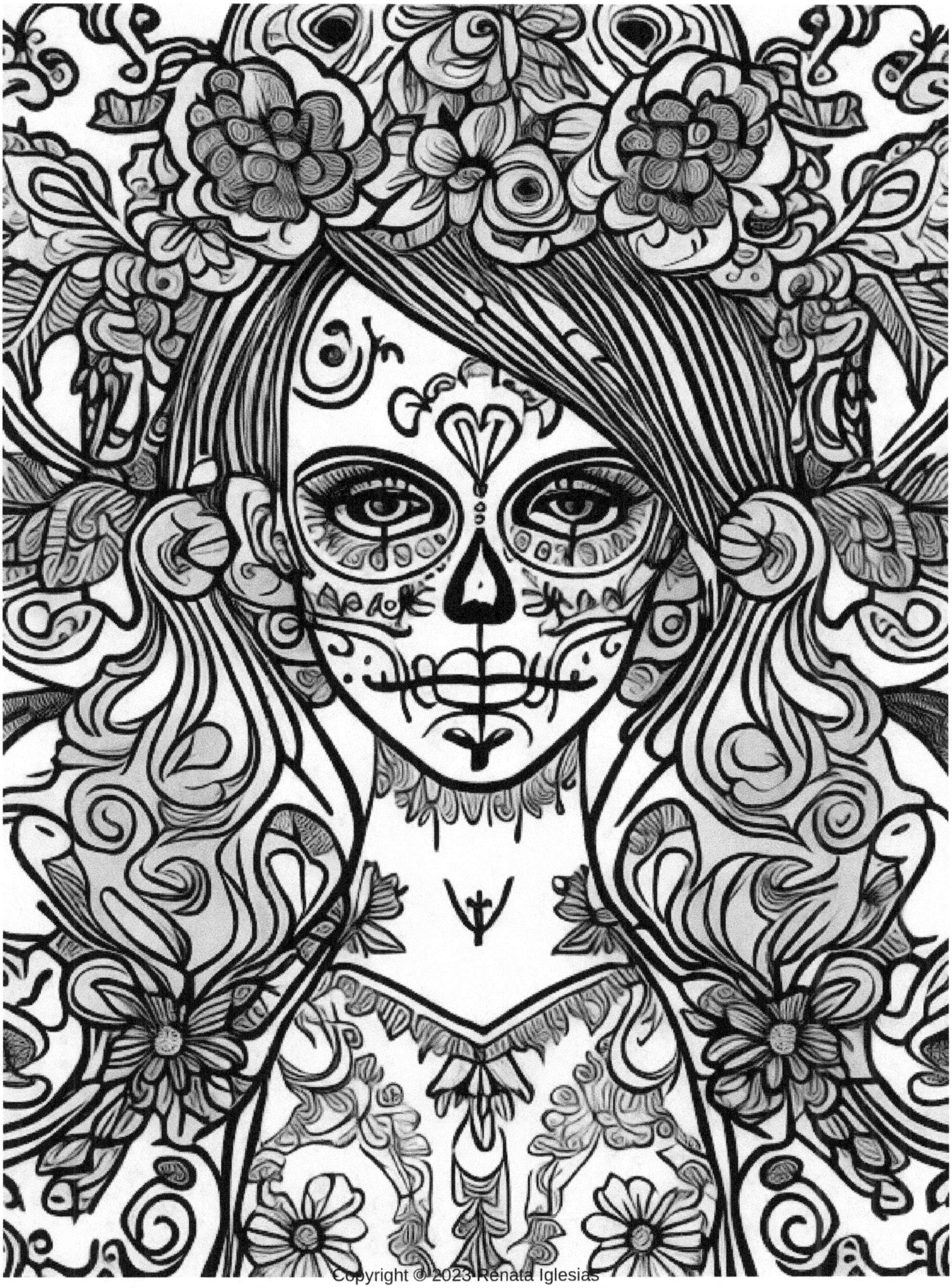

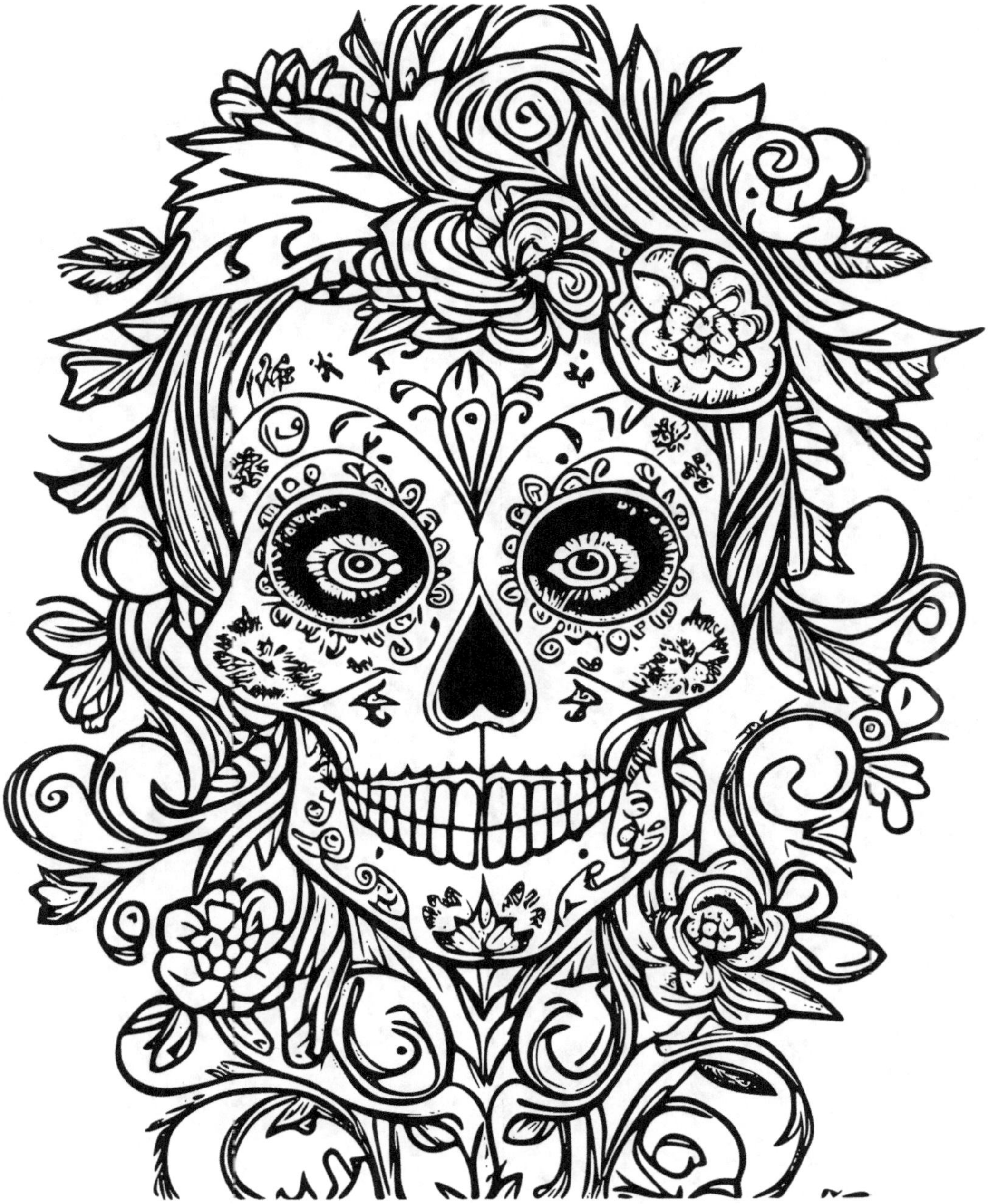

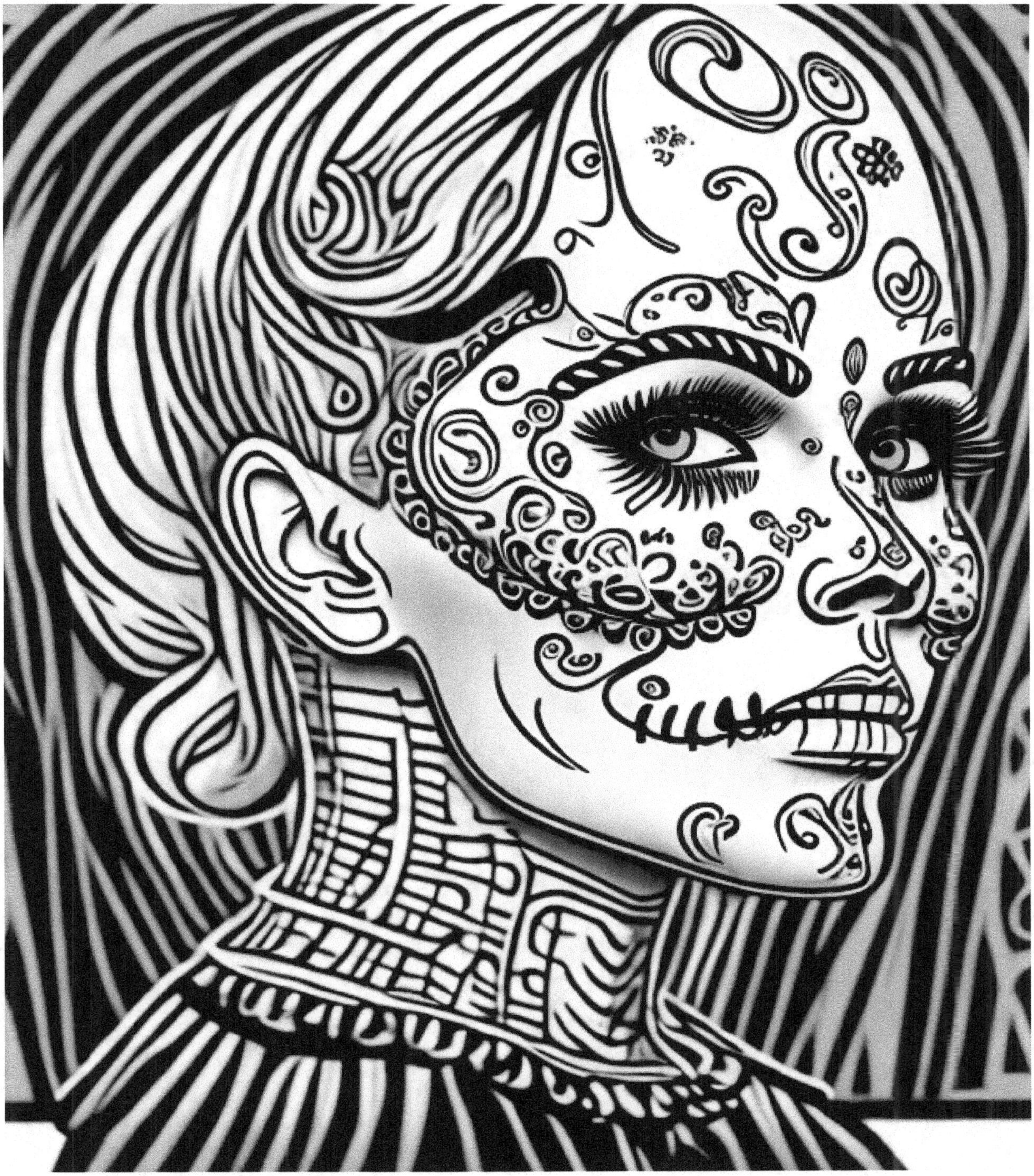

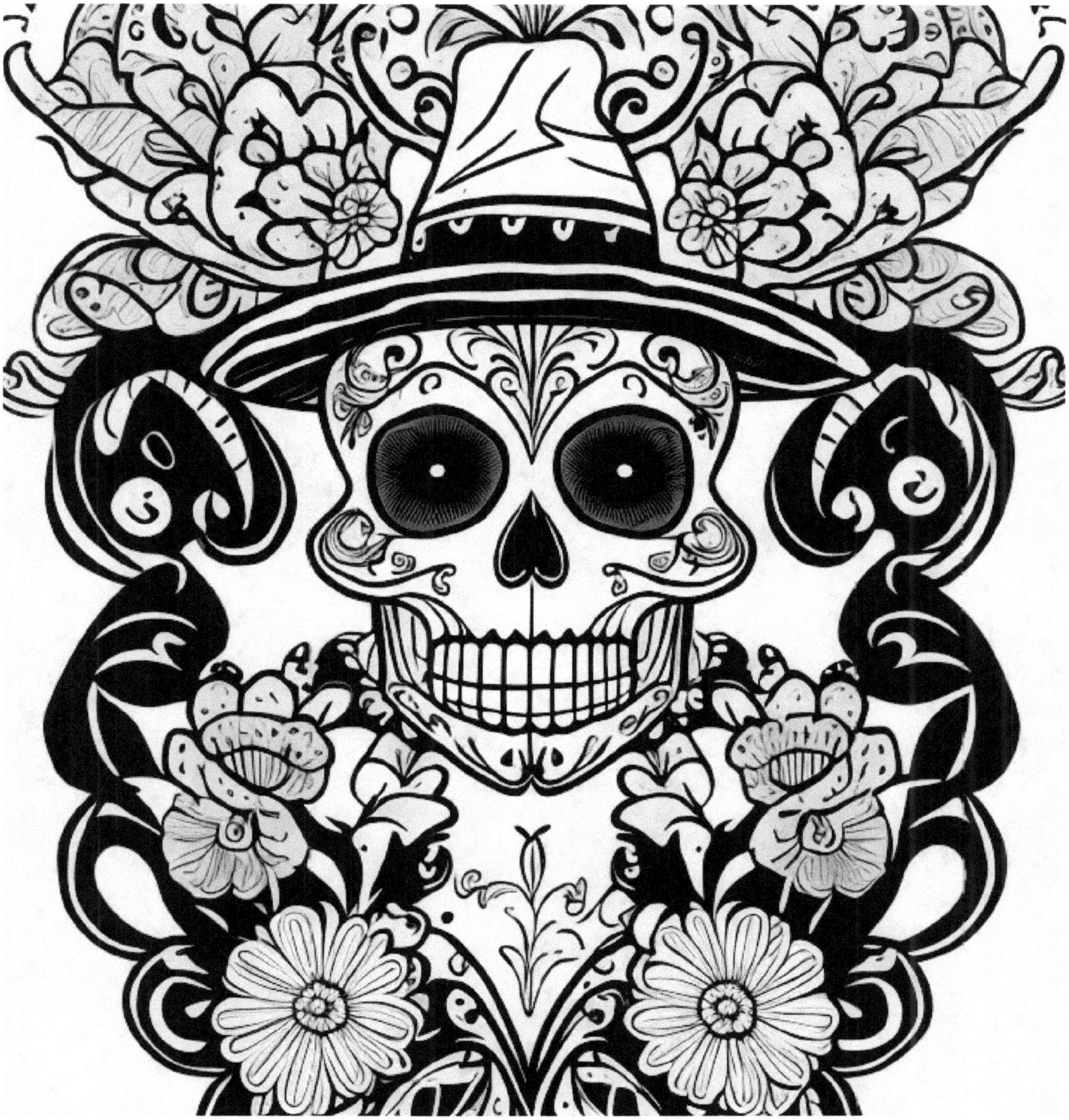

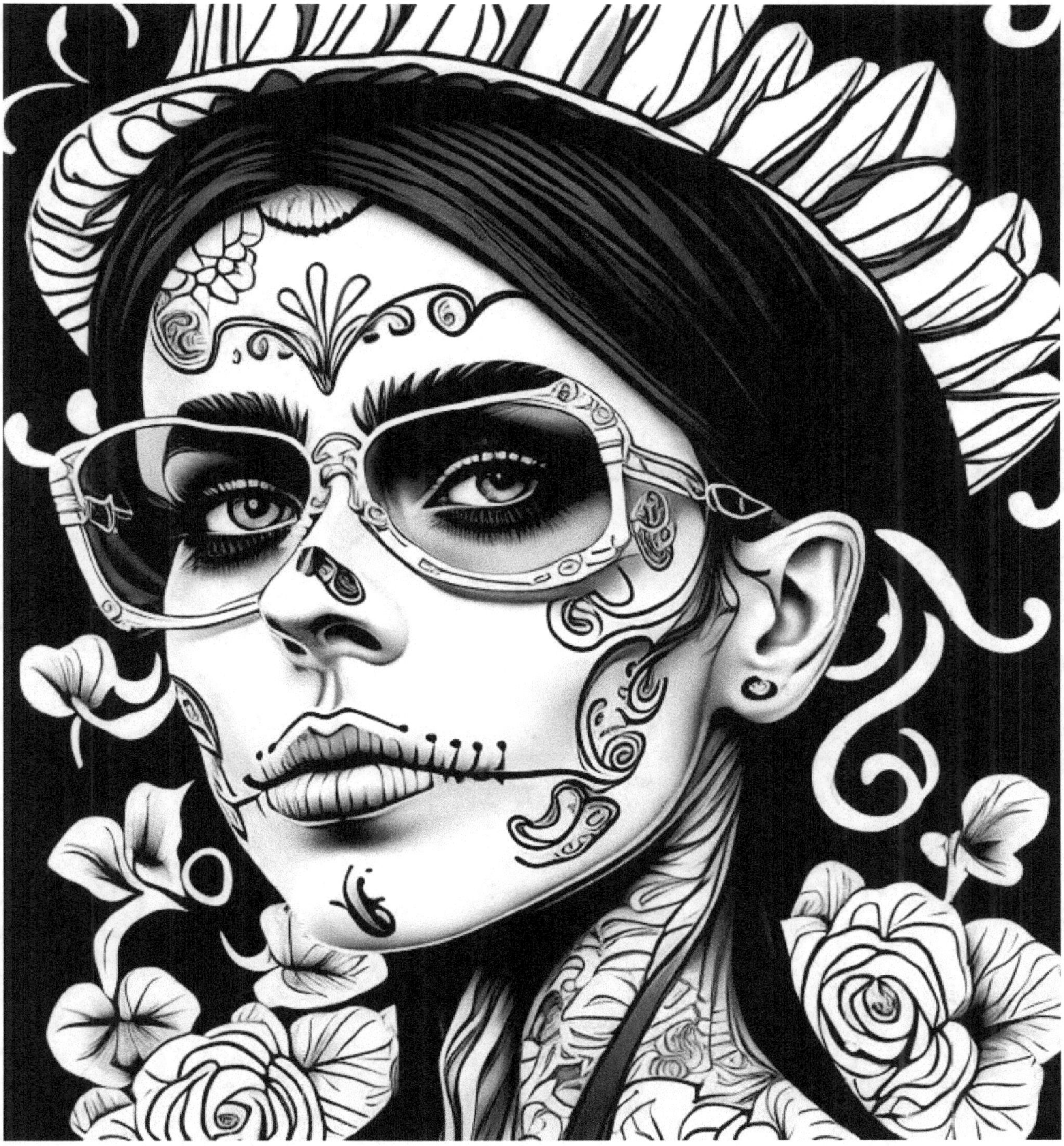

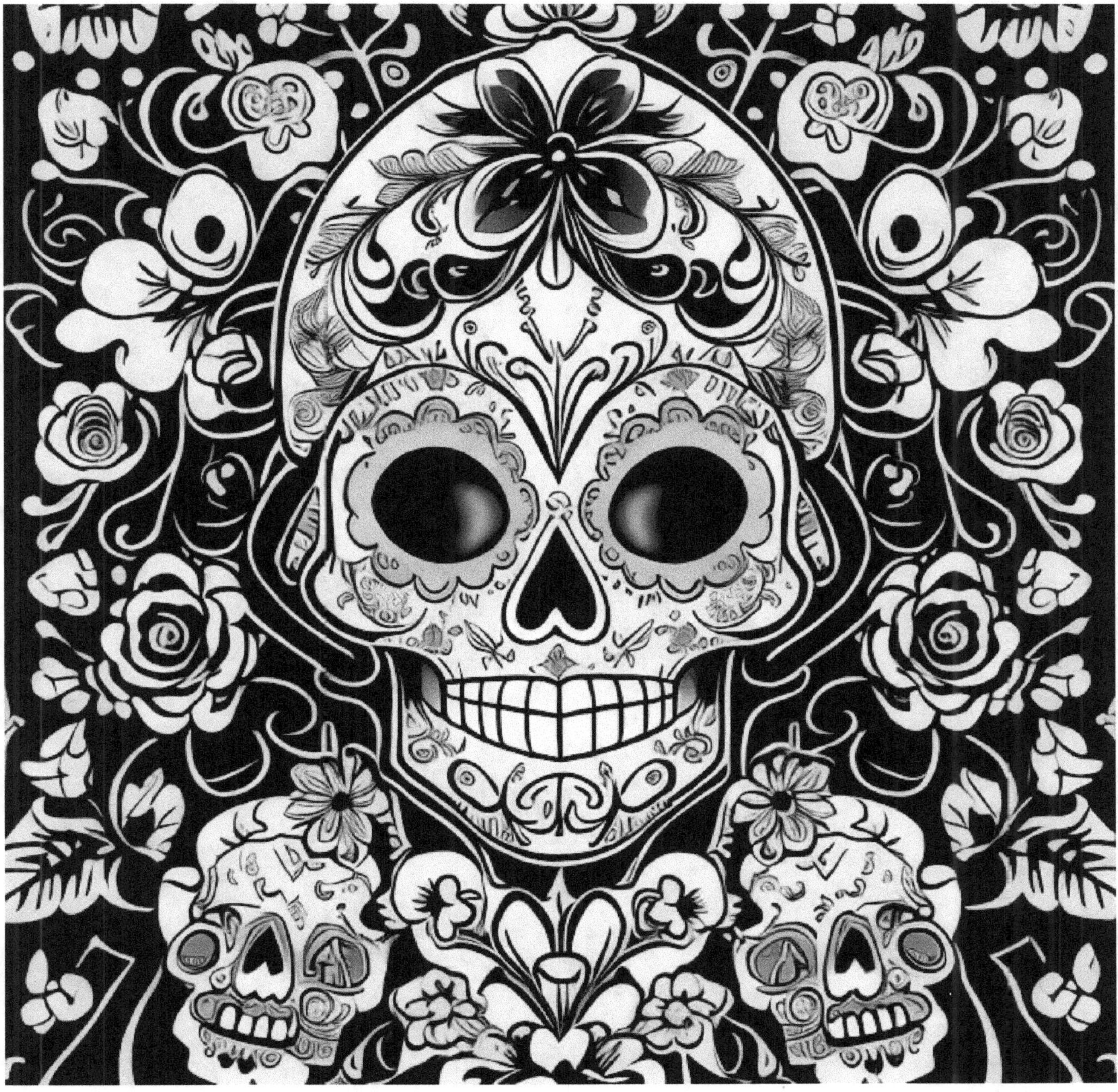

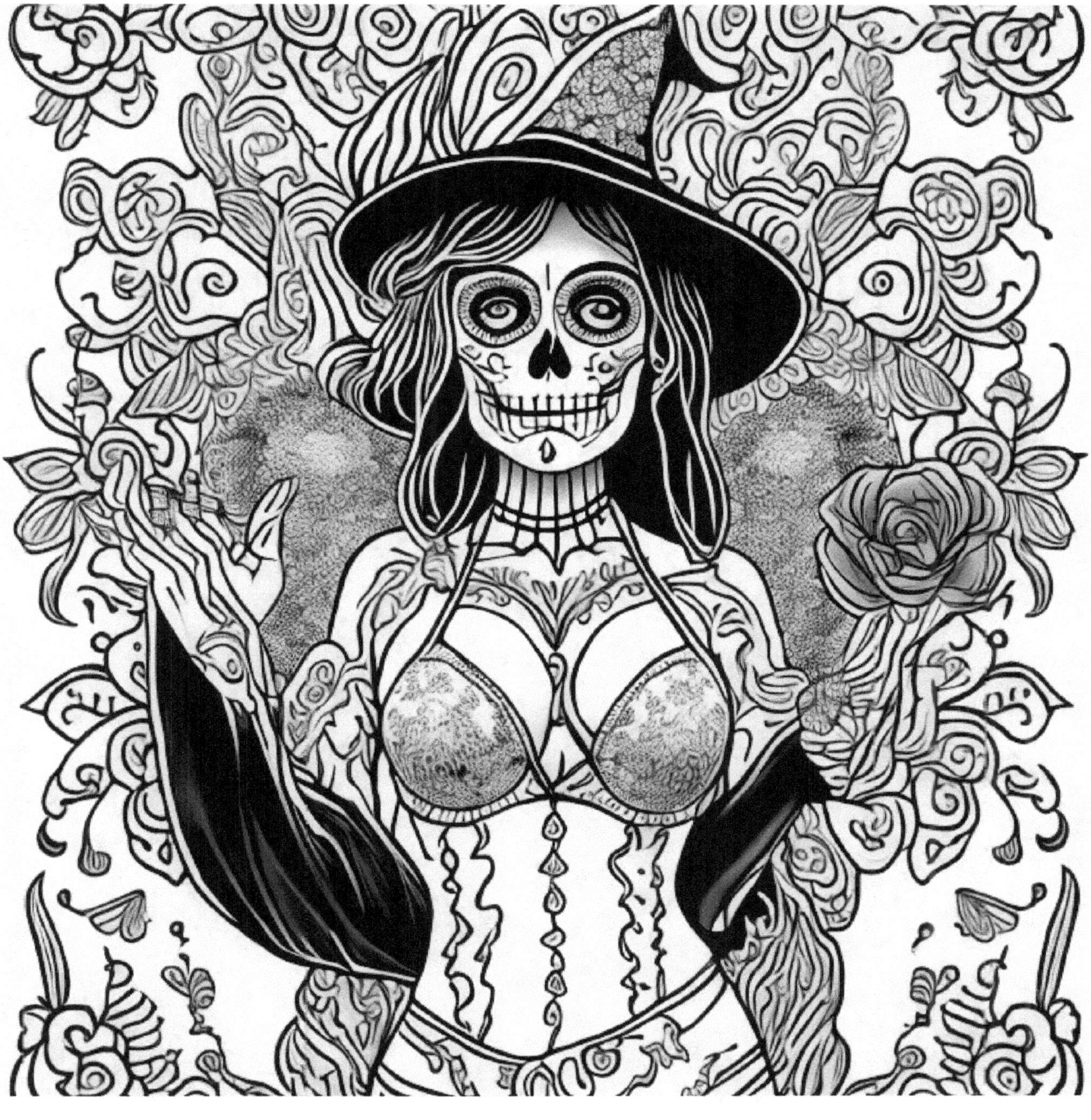

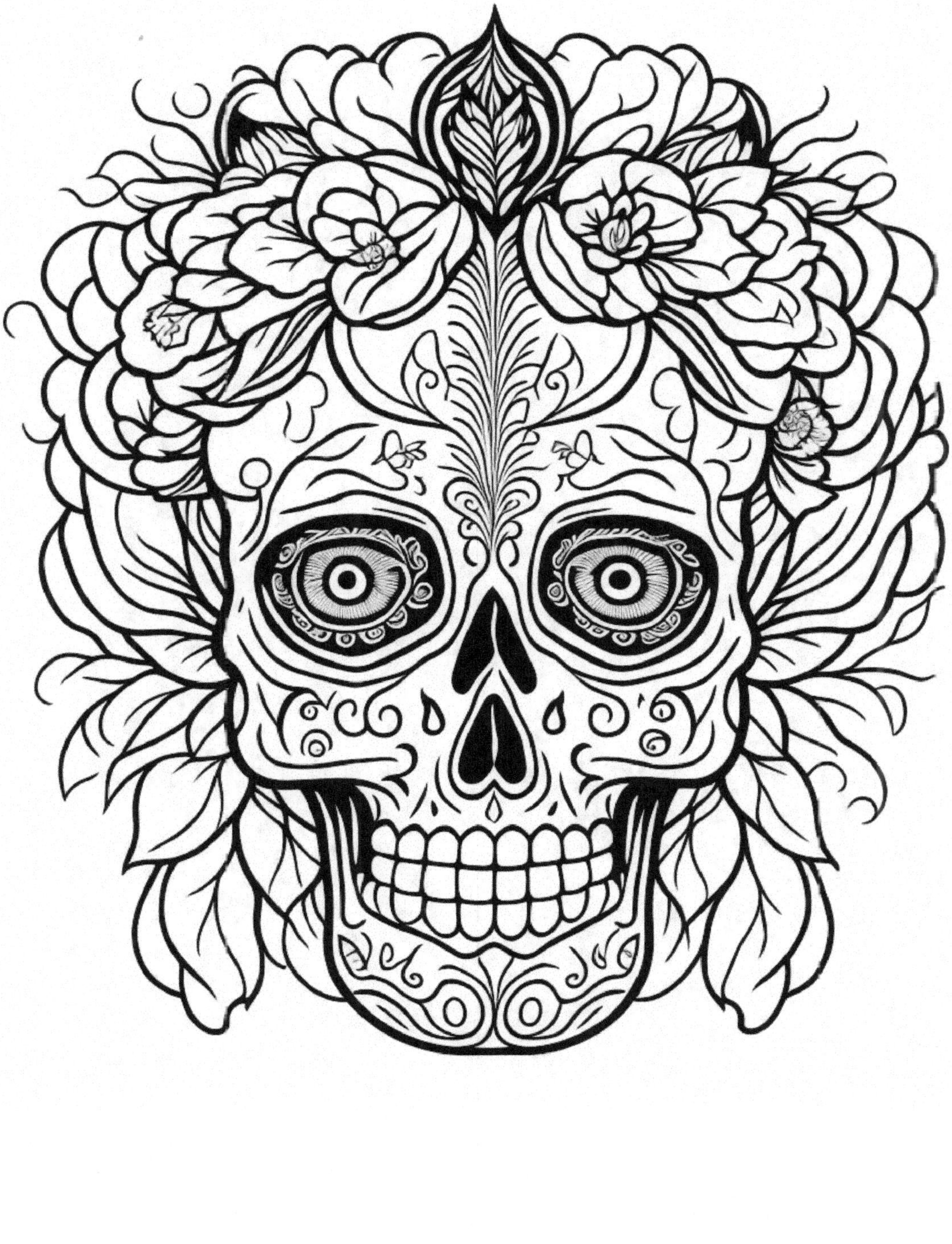

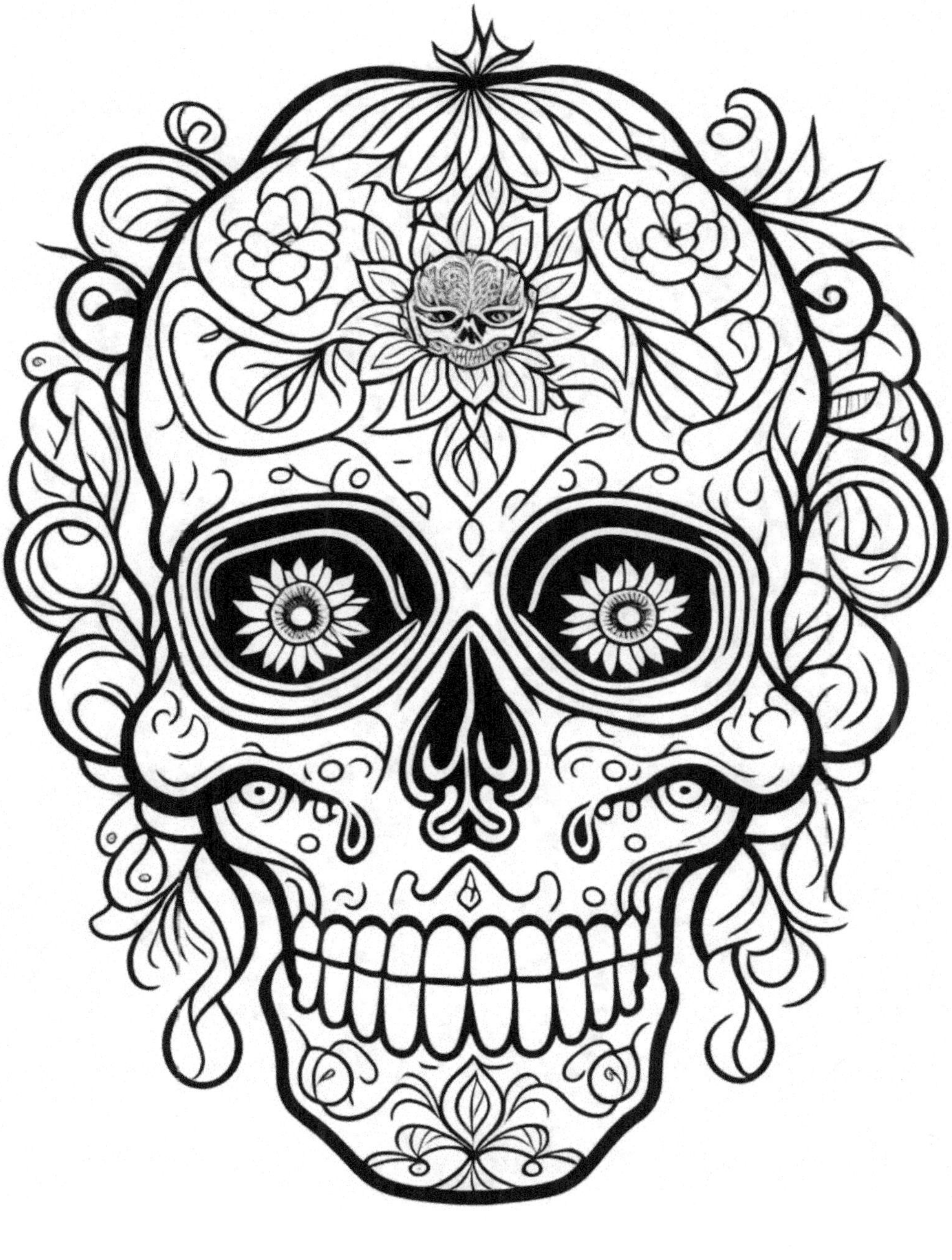

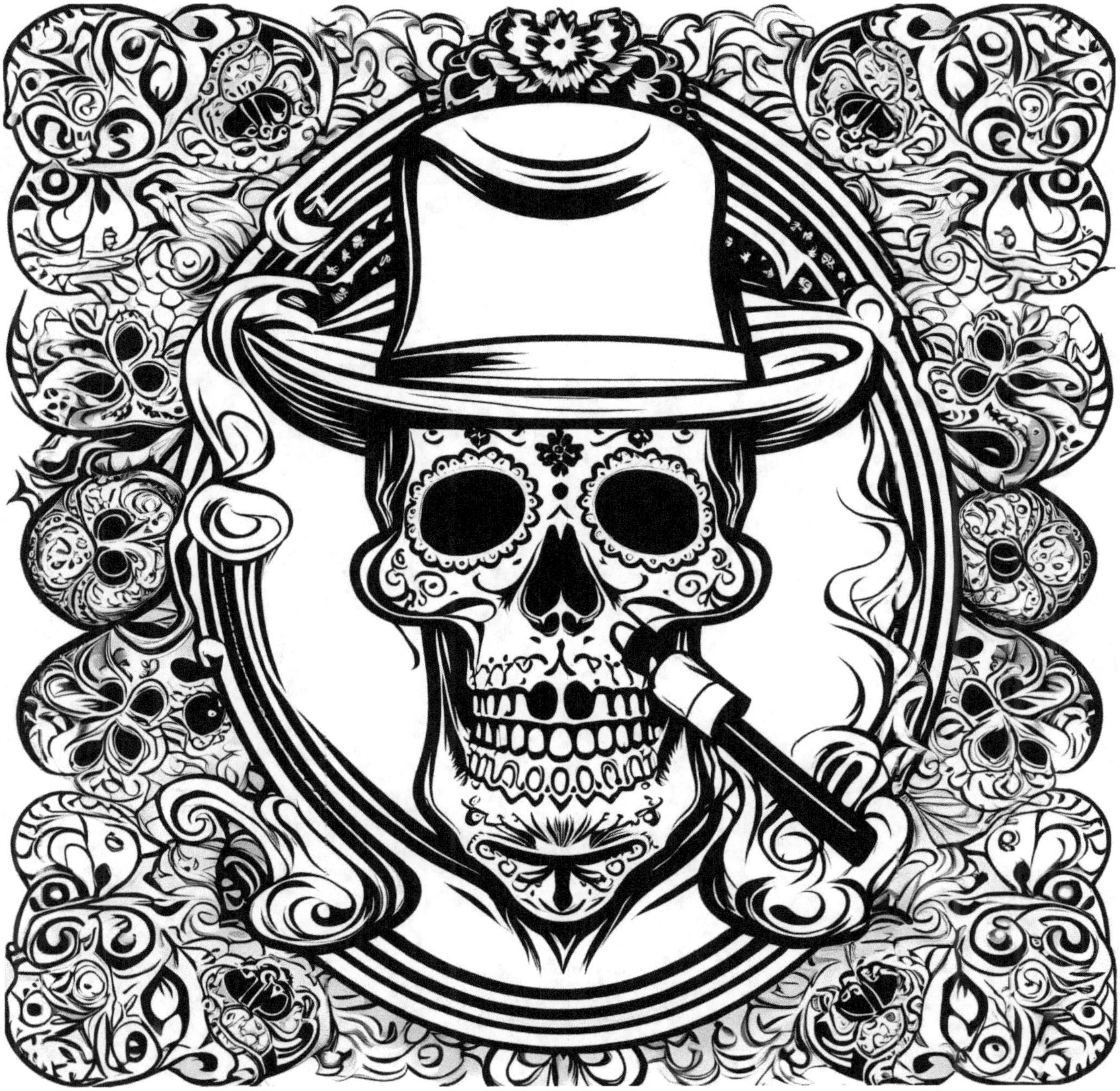

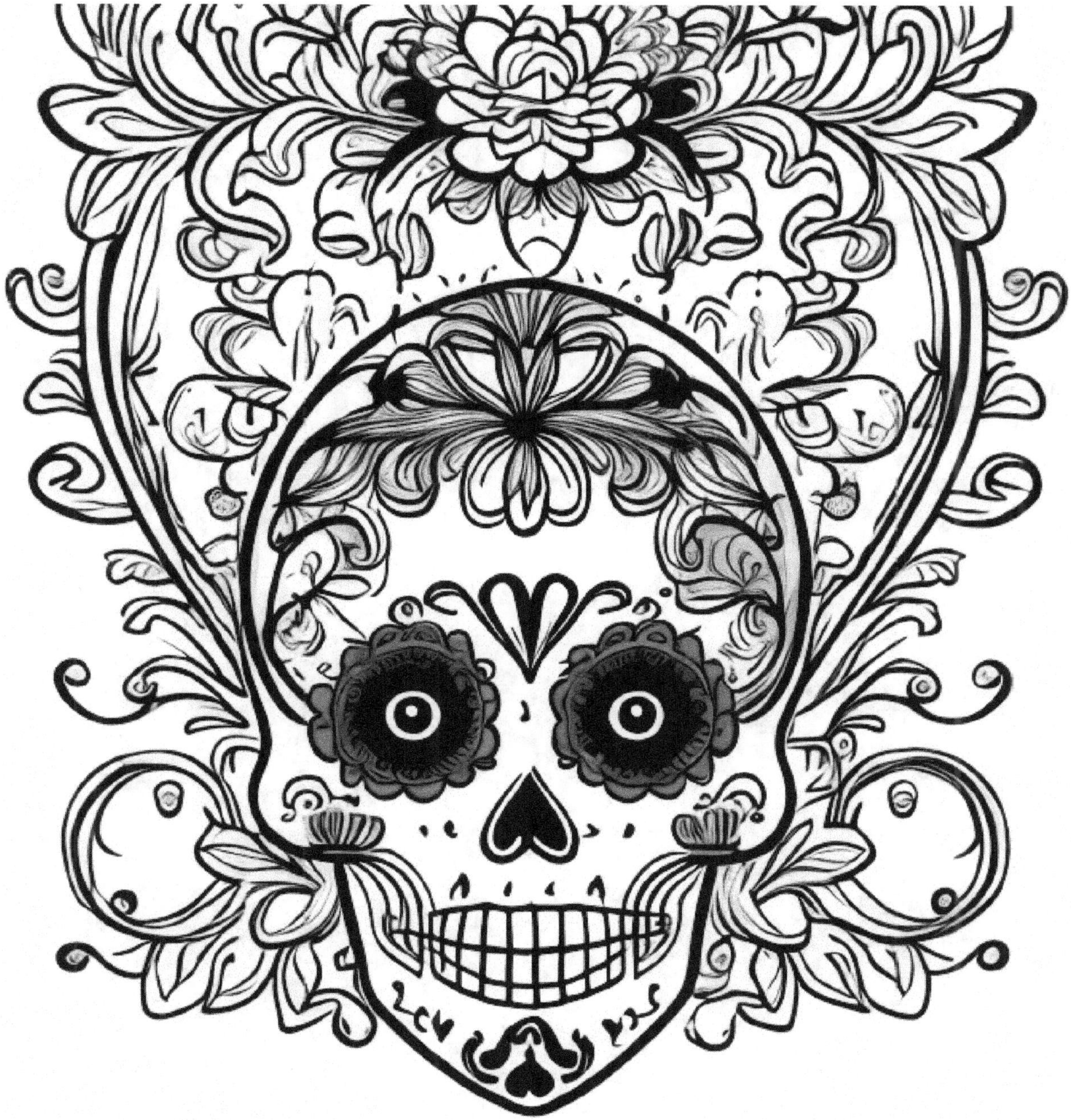

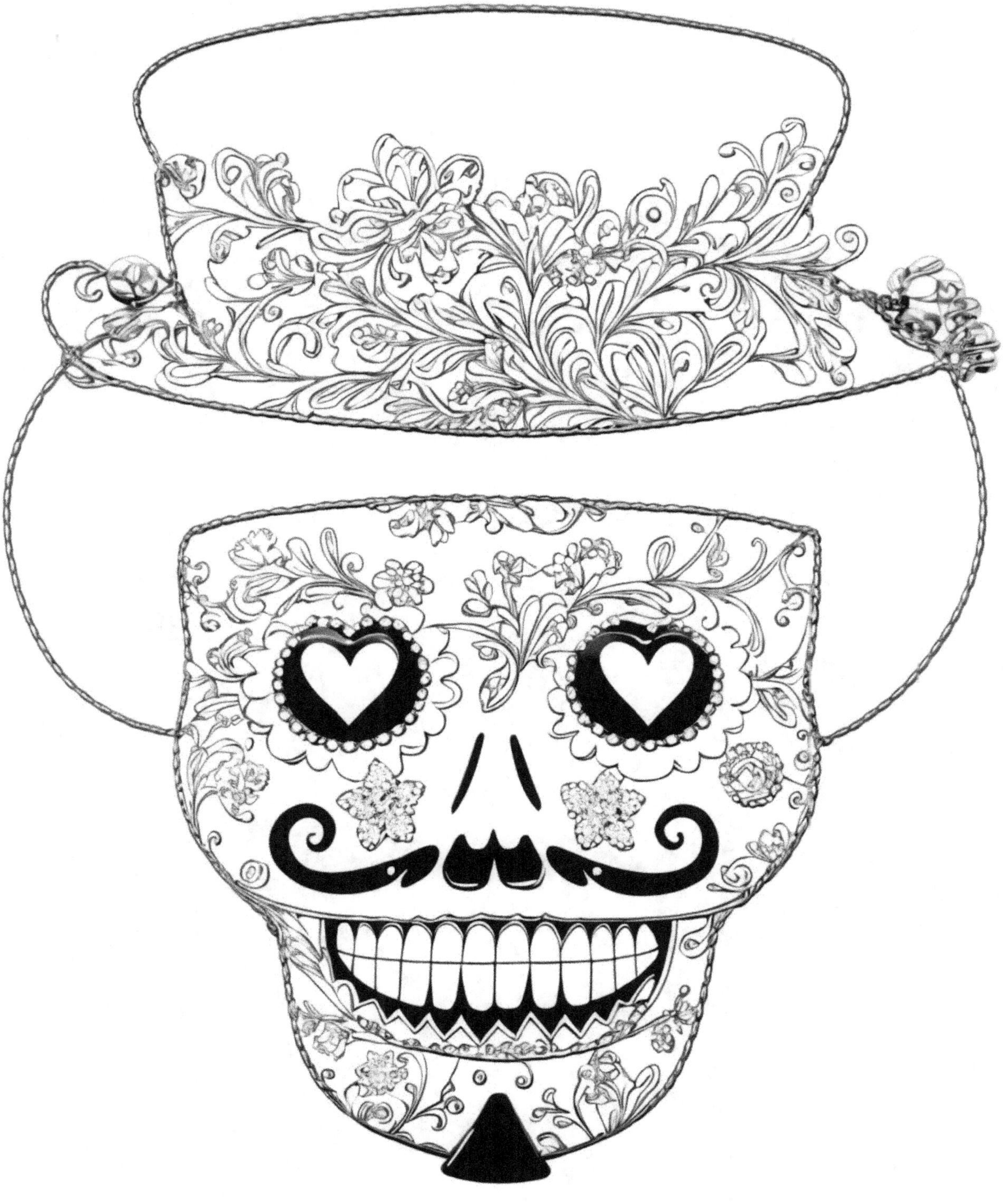

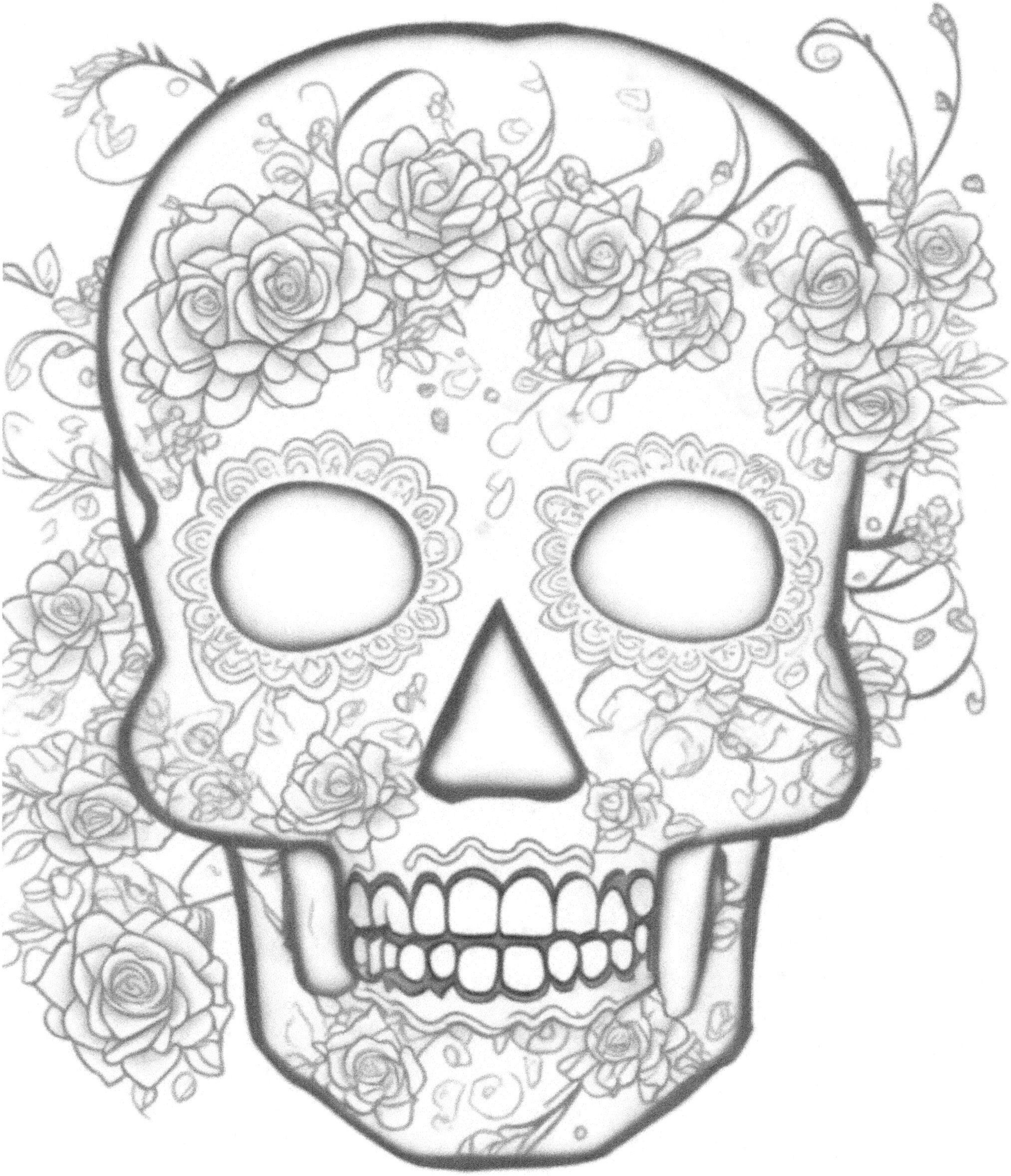

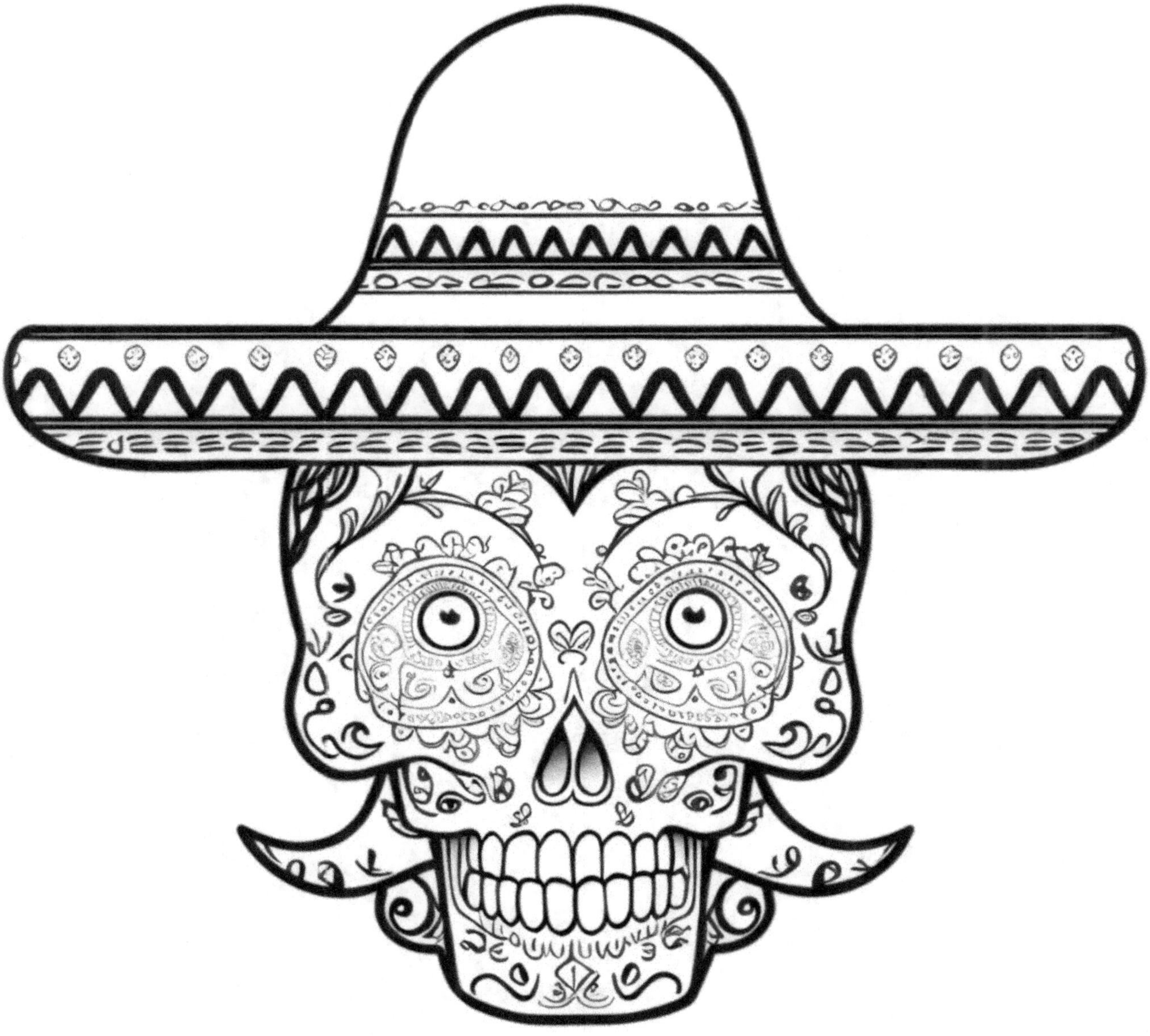

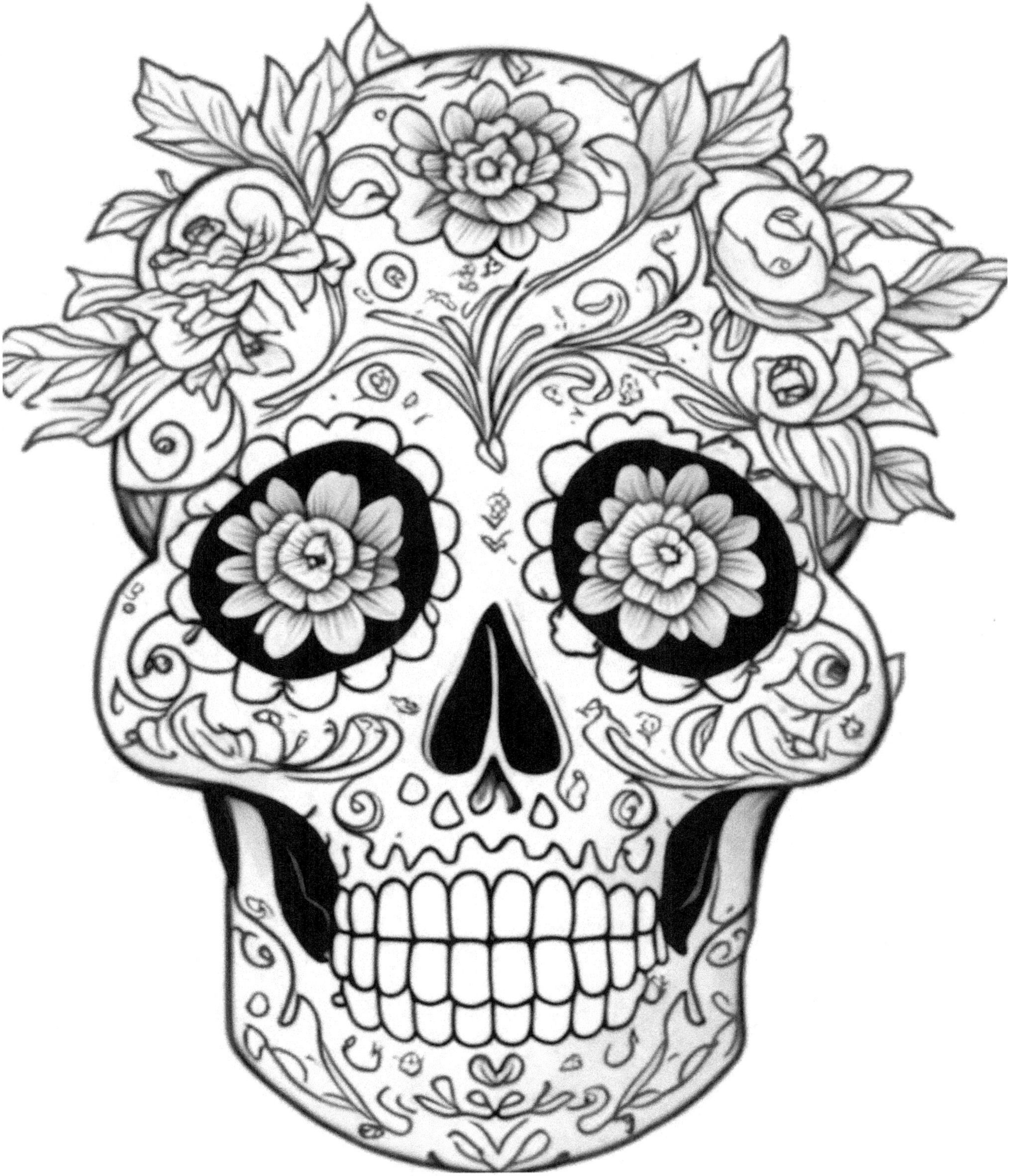

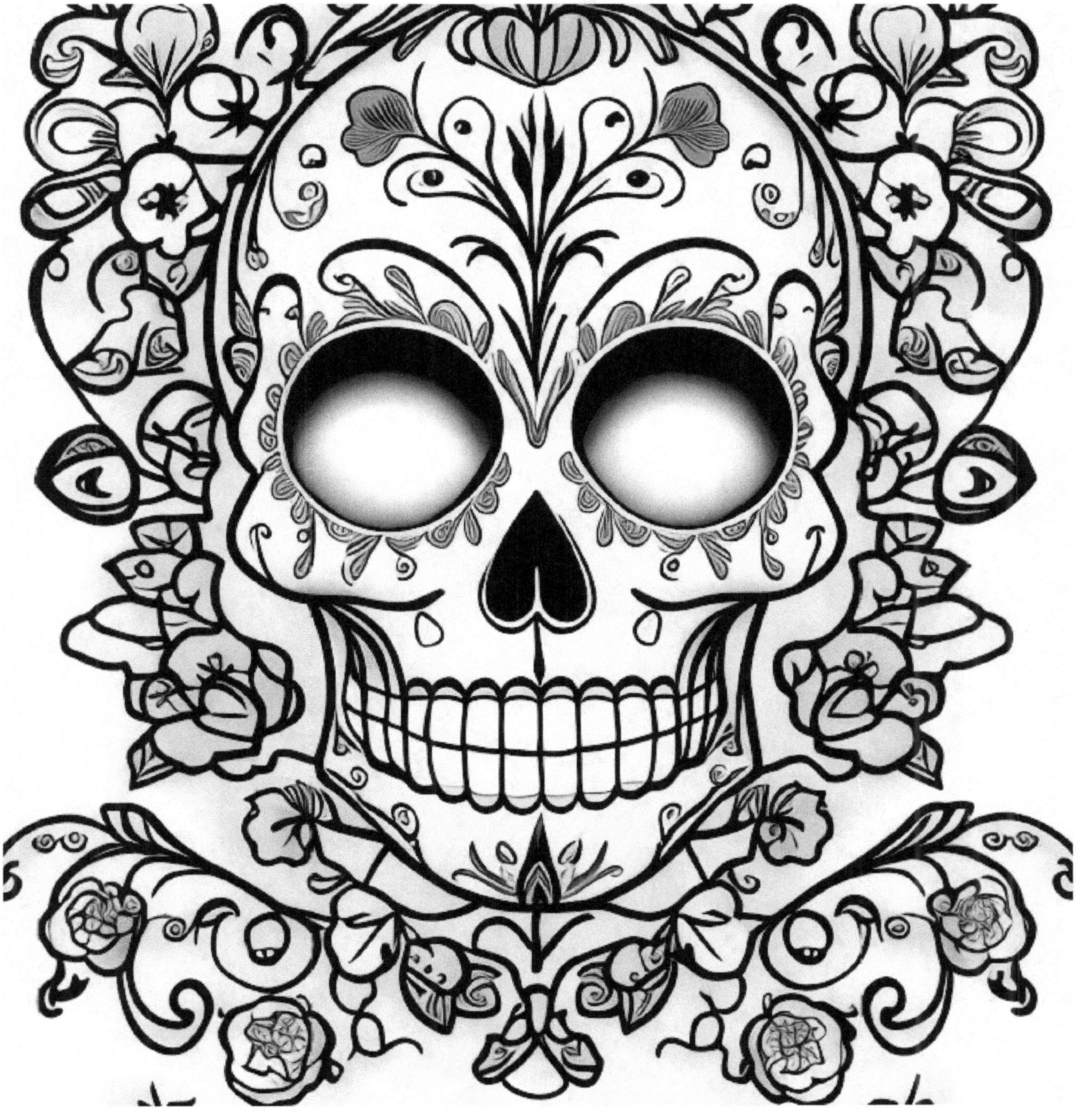

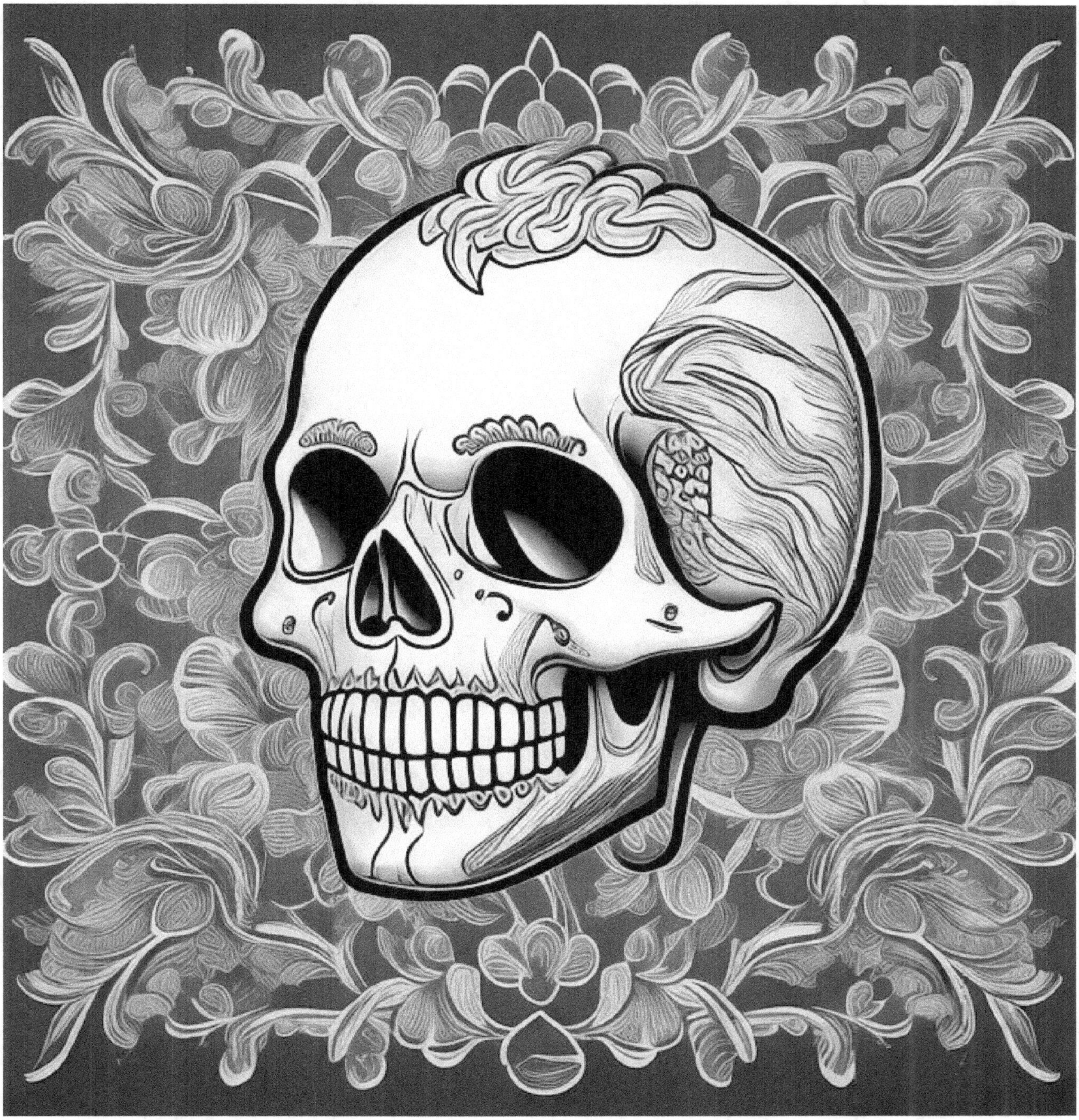

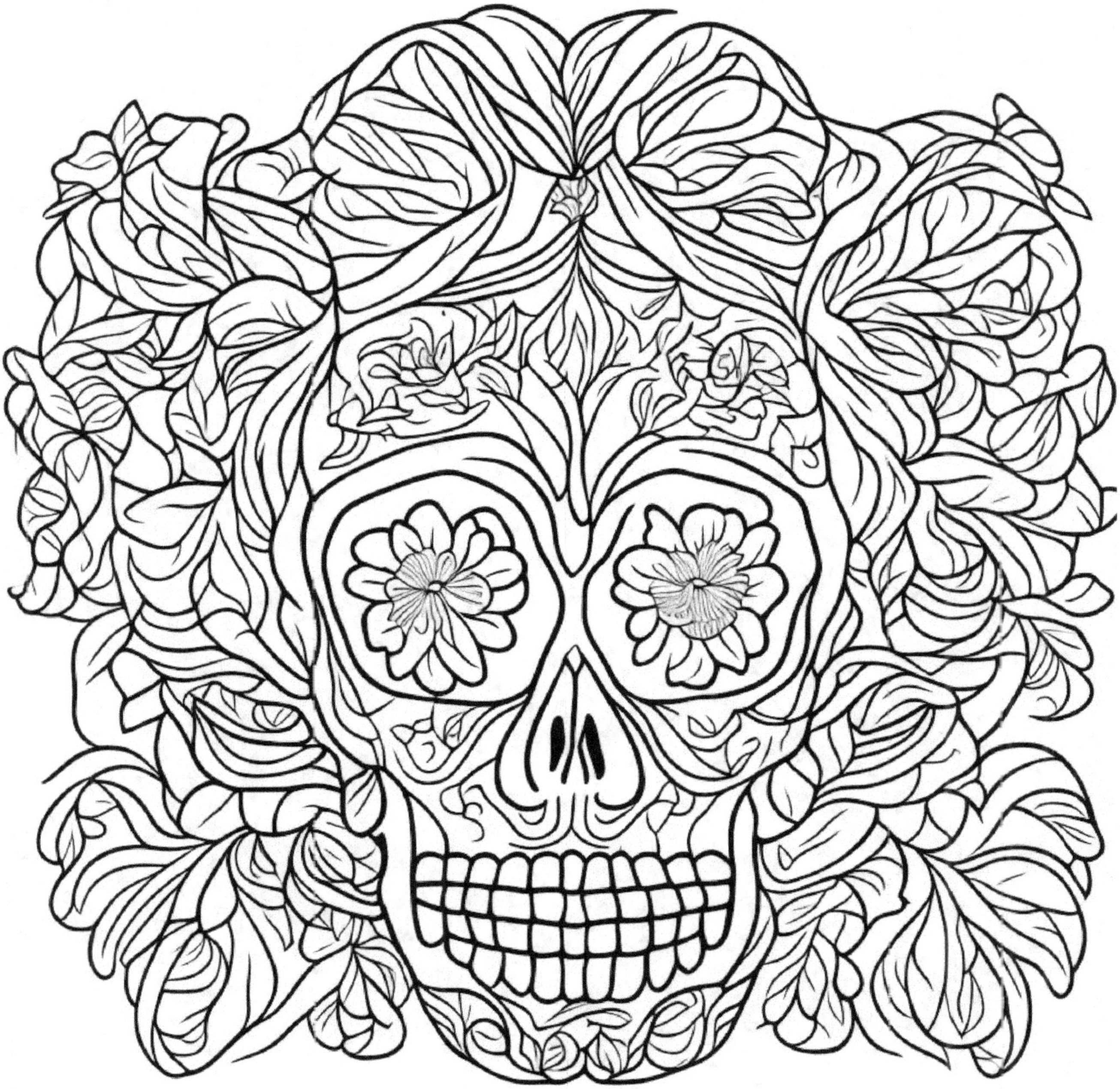

www.ingramcontent.com/pod-product-compliance
Lightning Source LLC
Chambersburg PA
CBHW082135290526
45794CB00008B/3045
* 9 7 9 8 8 5 1 3 6 8 6 8 4 *